CANCELLED

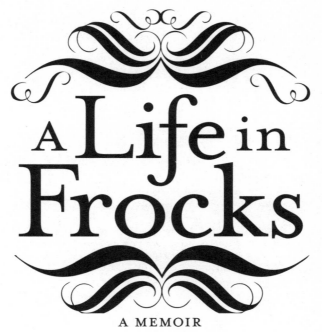

A MEMOIR

KELLY DOUST

illustrated by
ZOË SADOKIERSKI

Published in 2010 by Pier 9, an imprint of Murdoch Books Pty Limited.

Murdoch Books Australia
Pier 8/9
23 Hickson Road
Millers Point NSW 2000
Phone: +61 (0) 2 8220 2000
Fax: +61 (0) 2 8220 2558
www.murdochbooks.com.au

Murdoch Books UK Limited
Erico House, 6th Floor
93–99 Upper Richmond Road
Putney, London SW15 2TG
Phone: +44 (0) 20 8785 5995
Fax: +44 (0) 20 8785 5985
www.murdochbooks.co.uk

Publisher: Colette Vella
Editor: Amanda Cromer
Design and illustration: Zoë Sadokierski

Text © Kelly Doust 2010
Illustrations © Zoë Sadokierski 2010
The moral right of the author has been asserted.
Design © Murdoch Books Pty Limited 2010

Some names of people appearing in this book have been changed.

National Library of Australia Cataloguing-in-Publication entry
Doust, Kelly.
A life in frocks : a memoir / Kelly Doust.
ISBN 978-1-74196-844-6 (pbk.)
Doust, Kelly.
Women's clothing—Australia.
Fashion—Australia.
Fashion design—Australia.
746.920994

Printed by Hang Tai Printing Co. Ltd,China

For Olive,
who is at the very beginning,
and James

CONTENTS

INTRODUCTION

Several years ago, I approached *Vogue* for the first time with an idea I had for an article. Called 'A soundtrack to my life', it would be about how music inspires us, and has so inspired me over the years when it comes to deciding what to wear. I had to pinch myself when they said yes, and set to penning it straight away. I stayed up many long nights refining this story, finding it difficult to contain my enthusiasm for the subject to a mere eighteen hundred words in order for it to fit inside their 'Upfront' section. Indeed, I think it needed to be cut down quite a bit.

When the article came out (a version of it is included in this book, with *Vogue*'s kind permission), friends commented on how they were reminded of significant events or periods in their own life, and what they wore then; how it made them nostalgic for a long-forgotten time or place, or a long-lost boyfriend. They would get a dreamy, faraway look in their eyes which I loved to see, and a smile often played at their lips. One friend in particular, my savvy publishing colleague Catherine Milne, suggested I write an entire book about my fashion adventures (and many misadventures) for this reason.

This book did not start out as a memoir—it was meant to be a mixture of thoughts, fantasies and conversations with other women about clothes, with some of my own story woven in. But as I was writing it, I found it began to evolve into something more personal. As I cast my mind back, the memories kept assailing me; of occasions where clothes had coloured my experiences irrevocably. Experiences I was convinced that even the most stylish, sartorially disciplined among us had been through at some stage in their lives.

Even though *A Life in Frocks* is about my own story and dabbling in the joy of clothes from childhood to present, I hope it's one that many women will relate to or find comfort in. Almost all of us have a love/hate relationship with our bodies, and this ties in with fashion and how we so often use clothes to define us. It's a topic that bears more scrutiny: the universal preoccupation with what we wear, and why we wear it.

Fashionistas, would-be fashionistas, and those who fear or feel excluded from the mainstream love affair with fashion: this is for you. Because you don't need to be beautiful or thin, and you certainly don't need to be rich. You just have to have the 'divine obsession', as designer Vera Wang calls it—the pure love of clothes—and so much else will fall into place. For how many beautiful women are truly beautiful without any style, and how many women with a great degree of style, but not the money or the looks, are considered glamorous, or desirable, or even beauties anyway?

_⟨⟩ 1 ⟨⟩_

FOR THE LOVE OF CLOTHES

For as long as I can remember, I have been passionate about clothes. They are my first, and most enduring, love affair to date. Like many women, I adore the playfulness of fashion and its endless ability to transform us. I love the almost sacred ritual and drama of getting dressed; assuming different identities in different outfits and exploring the many facets of my personality through whatever I choose to wear, on any given day. But I also adore the irreverence of turning the totally expected on its head for the pure joy of discovering something new. My husband has accused me of being obsessed, and he's right: I'm simply addicted to clothes, as surely as if they were a drug.

Most of all, I love reading between the lines to figure out the myriad things that clothes say about us.

I read street-style blogs such as Jak & Jill, Garance Doré and The Sartorialist every day, and buy far too many glossy magazines, poring avidly over the details of proportion, cut, colour and embellishment. I watch television and film with one part focus on the costumes, one part focus on the plot, and soak up programs or movies about fashion with relish. I feel as if I spend half my life shopping (or thinking about shopping), and yet still find myself standing in front of a vast rack of items each morning in despair, thinking, *But I have nothing to wear!*

When I look through pictures taken of me at earlier stages in my life—wearing migraine-inducing prints and fire-engine-red curls during a retro-only phase at university, or flannelette courtesy of the grunge era in my teens—I feel pangs of acute embarrassment and occasionally let out an involuntary groan. But, at the same time, I can vividly remember how cool and fashion-forward I felt in that moment. I doubt there's a person alive who doesn't have the same ambiguous relationship with at least one outfit they've stepped out in before.

Over the years clothes have comforted me, given me confidence, lured love interests, made me invisible, secured jobs, aged me and given back my youth. They have beguiled, seduced and transfixed me with their siren song. And yes, they have betrayed me.

It's a testament to their immense power that clothes can be so many things, and sometimes all at once: armour, disguise, camouflage, fun, ironic, witty and over the top. Everyone knows the right outfit will send the right signal, but the wrong one can spell disaster, entirely ruining your day (or even, in Jane Austen's era at least, your life). Fashion has so much to say about our state of mind and our place in the world; where we're from and where we're going.

To say clothes are hugely important and intrinsic to our everyday selves is an understatement.

— 2 —

Peter Pan collars

The first outfit I can remember wearing was a dusky pink blouse with a Peter Pan collar and puffy sleeves, paired with maroon corduroy knicker-bockers. I must have been about five or six. A delightful combination made even more delightful by the fact that my brother, Jack, had a matching set in blue (this was before my second brother, born three or four years later, was even a glint in my father's eye). It was the very early eighties, after all, and together we wore this charming ensemble to the Open Day of Saint Augustine's, our new primary school. To complete the look, I sported black patent Mary Janes with white frill-topped socks. Lord knows what my brother's equivalent was. As we dressed that morning, I remember staring at us side by side in the mirror, positively preening. We looked *the business.*

I often think of those outfits and wonder why, as children of the opposite sex, Jack and I were dressed the same (even given the concession to pink and blue). Were they gifts from an aunt or grandmother, saved to be worn for this special occasion? Or was it simply easier for my mother, Maria, to select matching sets during a harried

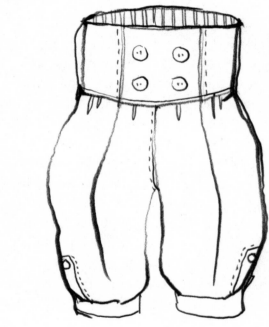

knicker
bockers

Peter
Pan

shopping trip? Why, indeed, does anyone dress their children alike, given that they're entirely separate individuals? Is it that, as pre-pubescent, barely formed people, our true nature is still so indecipherable, or mutable? Maybe it's no more complex than a subconscious search for order. No-one can deny that matching outfits just *go*. They look neat together. And it's no surprise that my parents grew up listening to The Beatles, The Supremes, The Jackson Five, and all those other boy bands and girl groups who made matching look hip.

But back to Open Day ... Standing shyly on the footpath while my mother fetched something from our beaten-up cream Mercedes, we met twins Carla and Bianca for the first time. Also dressed in matchy-matchy fashion, they wore long-sleeve polo-necks with bell-bottomed cords—one in chocolate brown, the other in orange-red—with Karen Carpenter hair, longish, shiny brown bobs cut in a way that perfectly framed their freckled, angelic faces. Those lovely twins resembled the captivating women I watched in disco-ball-lit music videos on television, *sans* microphones. In that instant I developed an aching fashion crush. *Damn you, knickerbockers,* I thought, and began plotting ways to destroy them. Maybe if I tripped over on the gravel I could take out the knees?

From that point on, I felt as if I were on a treasure hunt to find just the right outfit for every occasion. Although I wasn't yet able to articulate it, I felt convinced that garments formed the foundation of my character (and the character of the people around me) with what they hid and revealed. Clothes were the key to unlocking so many mysteries, if only I could understand what they were trying to say ...

As a child I was fascinated by the adult world that clothes represented. Like so many women, I remember watching my mother prepare to go out for the evening; blow-drying her hair with a rounded brush into a Farrah Fawcett circa *Charlie's Angels* flick, dabbing the stopper from a bottle of Chanel N°5 on her wrists and behind the ears, clipping on some costume earrings and slipping a new dress over her small frame. She would slide her feet into glamorous cork wedges and grab a delicate clutch (containing only lipstick) before instructing the babysitter about bedtimes and kissing us goodnight. Then she and my father, Robert (oh so dashing in his wide-lapelled suit), walked arm-in-arm out the front door. It all seemed terribly grown-up, and I longed to be older so I could go through my own dressing and *toilette* ritual.

I was, it seems, a precocious child who wanted to be taken seriously, not to be sent to bed; I loved being forgotten at the table while my parents and their friends bantered about sex and marriage and business over boozy dinner parties. If allowed to stay up, I took it all in, and occasionally inter-jected with what I thought to be witty repartee. Sometimes, I even snuck from my room to sit at the top of the landing and secretly listen in to their conversations until my eyelids grew heavy and I succumbed to sleep. Being the eldest of three, I longed to be thought of as more than just a child, and felt bitterly disappointed when sent off to play with my two younger brothers—away from the scintillating discus-sion. I hated the feeling I was missing out.

My parents taught me to read from a very early age. My father—a bricklayer-turned-builder who had been expelled from London's prestigious Harrow School (where he attended as a scholarship student) at the age of fourteen for smoking—always carried about him a gruff, disappointed air. But he was passionate on the subject of education, and had high hopes for us all. His strong-willed stance on books instilled in me a love of reading, a habit which went hand-in-hand with my impatience to grow up and get on with the business of real living. Books led me, vicariously, through so many adult experiences.

In novels I discovered so much about human failings and motivations; about sex and love and jealousy and drama; joy and tragedy, and what you wore on either occasion. Long before I understood what the lesson really meant, I learned of the foolishness of youth and how it is so often wasted on the young, secreting pearls of wisdom such as this about my person—a few more pieces of a riddle waiting to be solved.

I also developed clear images in my mind of what my favourite characters looked like; how they dressed, how they carried themselves, and how they wore their hair. I sat in front of the mirror at my youthful dressing table, trying on their speech and mannerisms, waving a chopstick posed as a 1920s cigarette holder. I raided my mother's make-up drawer for deep red lipstick and her jewellery box for other feminine accoutrements, imagining grown men and admiring women wilting at my feet.

The power of refinement, effected through clothing and other means of enchantment, had been made clear to me through books. Cassandra and Rose, those lovely sisters from Dodie Smith's *I Capture the Castle*, might have been cripplingly poor, but they knew how to have fun with a few old frocks and some green dye, attracting the attention of the rich brothers next door. Those girls had ingenuity! Sparky Flora Poste of *Cold Comfort Farm*, the first Mrs de Winter in *Rebecca*, and Heathcliff's Cathy in *Wuthering Heights*; these were women, both lovely and terrible, who were worth swooning over. I often dreamed I could be them, sashaying through the rooms of their gothic English homes in my mind.

Once I turned twelve, my father started feeding me books well beyond my years. The first was John Irving's *A Prayer for Owen Meany*, quickly followed by every other novel Mr Irving had written up to that point, including *The World According to Garp*, *The Hotel New Hampshire* and *The Cider House Rules*. If you've read them you will know they cover such lurid topics as incest, drug addiction and the vagaries of love and war. But for a child discovering them for the first time, they were also poignant and achingly beautiful. I was astonished by the depths of what humans were capable of, and began to look at the world around me with a fresh perspective.

My reading lust consumed me, and I'd sometimes get through ten or fifteen books during the two-week school holidays; from crime novels to biographies, travel narratives to thrillers, occasionally interspersed with a bit of *Dolly* magazine's fiction or the *Sweet Valley High* series (striving to mimic the preppy teen glamour of their modern-day heroines). I worked my way through classics old and new, particularly enjoying tales of bright young things in their prime, and the dangers that threatened to extinguish them in the novelists' search for poetic justice. From Jane Austen to Kerouac, via F. Scott Fitzgerald, Nancy Mitford and Evelyn Waugh, I lamented the end of the Jazz Age, the fifties, and every other era worth living in where people used dress as a form of rebellion and unapologetic self-expression, with an old-world glamour I felt I was unlikely to experience in my lifetime.

I searched for parallels within my own limited experience, looking vainly for a sense of style and history in the leather and denim garb, held together with safety pins, of the mohawked punks who roamed the streets of the inner-city area I grew up in. Sadly, there were no debutantes or dashing young men (referring to each other as 'old sport' or 'old man') to be found.

My fascination with the natty threads described in my favourite tomes led me to my next love: magazines. I would pore over *Dolly* and back issues of *The Face* (which I'd found in a box on the street, left by neighbours for the council to collect) for all-important clues to the adult I imagined I would become. A romantic lead in my own coming-of-age drama, sparklingly witty and sincerely stylish.

The only objection from my parents was their worry I was spending too much time inside. If they sent me outside to 'go play', I would simply hide the book or magazine I was reading under the waistband of my jeans, and finish it on the swings of our local park. It was left to my brothers to tear about constructing cubby houses, collecting tadpoles, or mulberries from the old tree—activities sometimes too tempting for even me to resist—while I wished myself into Enid Blyton's *Famous Five* series, *The Magic Faraway Tree*, or *The Chronicles of Narnia*.

I studied the looks captured on models' faces in magazines, and practised them while catching the bus to school or playing Monopoly (rather than bridge or whist, the favoured pastime of the characters from my beloved books), often prompting someone to ask, 'What's wrong?' upon clocking my gormless expression in an unsuccessful attempt to look lovelorn, or courageous, or blissful.

On one visit to our local park, my brother and I found a discarded porn magazine on a bench. My brain was unable to compute the message it was trying to convey, for none of the people within were wearing clothes I could 'read'. I remember feeling puzzled by a picture of a man wearing nothing but a black top hat, shaggy black curls tumbling out to frame his face. Of all the nudes in that magazine, it's his vacant-eyed visage that has stuck in my mind—no doubt because he was the only one wearing anything ... and what an unusual choice of headgear he made when he did!

Books and clothes were my twin obsessions, but it wasn't until I secured my first job at age twelve—washing the soupy buckets at a local florist after school and on the weekends— that I had the means to buy my own preferred books and clothing, and stop raiding my mother's closet or donning hand-me-downs from a favoured aunt.

I remember trips to my local charity store, clipped-out images in hand, on the hunt for dusty items I could buy for a song with my meagre wage (nay, a small fortune) which resembled those I saw in my beloved fashion magazines. And, oh, how I loved Molly Ringwald in that 1980s classic, *Pretty in Pink*. Far from turning my nose up at the musty smell of St Vincent de Paul and its second-hand clothes ('The smell of death,' as it was referred to by one of my friends), I was fascinated by the life these clothes had already lived. I conjured elaborate images in my mind of the events each item had seen, whole episodes explaining the arc of their existence—from a new frock hanging on a shop rack, to its various outings, before it eventually ended up in my hot little hands. *What things we will do together,* I would excitedly think.

I was a bit of an odd bod as a child, and even more so as a teenager. We moved around often and I was always the new kid in the neighbourhood or classroom. I learned to be adaptable, and studied people ever so closely, but never really fitted in. A class clown in one school, a mouse in the next; or popular for exactly one term ... I often had the opportunity to try on new personalities for size, just to see if they fit.

I remember spending weeks agonising over what to wear for 'mufti'—casual-clothes days—at school. I did thorough research beforehand, talking to the cool girls for a clue as to what they would come donned in, but when the day finally arrived I always felt as if I had got it wrong. I would walk to the bus stop that morning with a spring in my step, resplendent in all my technicoloured glory, wearing hot pink high-top L.A. Gear sneakers, denim cut-offs, and a jaunty striped sleeveless tee ... only to get to school to find those same popular girls wearing simple white tank tops, flat Reeboks with white laces and beige Bermuda shorts. It would take a while for it to sink in, this concept of fitting in, as my natural flair for standing out thanks to unusual clothes was becoming a theme.

Luckily, a succession of school uniforms mostly saved me from public humiliation at the hands of some of the disasters I invented: I'm talking about the red bat-wing tee with high-waisted, puffy legged acid-wash denim jeans (Grade 6), or the ruffled, violet valance-like top and leggings, fringe teased into a solid wall above my forehead with the rest of my hair scrunched up into a puffy 'do which looked as though it had been strapped, helmet-like, to my head (Grade 7). Despite the ridicule I received, I remained determined to persevere with fashion: I simply loved clothes too much to give in.

I don't remember the light-bulb moment in which the realisation occurred, but it just always seemed obvious that clothes were clues; understanding them meant unlocking the secrets of the strange, sometimes vexing behaviour of those around me, and establishing my own identity. When you're forced to negotiate new terrain (and remember, everything is new when you're young) it helps to have a roadmap, and a plan.

Costume was my roadmap, my plan.

— ⁓ 3 ⁓ —

DREAMING APPAREL

Ask me today what my perfect outfit is and I'll tell you this:

A fabulously frothy tutu in the shade of sea foam, made from layers and layers of soft tulle. It nips in tight at the waist—a stretch satin band in a darker green—and blooms delightfully outwards, ending above the knee with artfully dishevelled edges falling over silky, translucent grey footless tights. On top, I'm wearing a pale pink bodysuit with tiny flower detail stitched into the fabric—not unlike a pretty spencer. And a shrunken cashmere cardigan, powder blue, with intricate beading and see-through sequins adorning the lapels. Around my neck is a fine silver chain and charm—a tiny, pastel-blue-enamelled peace sign, or perhaps a mini Eiffel Tower layered over a longer Tiffany & Co. key pendant. My feet are shod in handmade silver ballet slippers, and slung over my right shoulder is a ruched, dove-grey bag made from the finest kidskin. My hair is up, parted to the right, in a messy chignon with stray strands curling about my ears. My make-up, minimal.

What does it say? *Life is beautiful.* In this playfully romantic outfit, the following could not, would not, occur:

* any flash of anger resulting in sharp words to my husband or child;
* a misunderstanding with a friend that leaves me in tears;
* an encounter with an untrustworthy business contact that makes me feel manipulated and unnerved;
* a phone call containing bad news about a beloved friend or family member;
* road rage involving some hoon in a ute who cuts me off in traffic; or,
* an accident involving my favourite lamp, the floor, and a million shards of porcelain.

But the following *would* occur:

- ✤ a delightful, rollicking picnic in the park with our friends and children;
- ✤ phone calls bearing good news from my publisher;
- ✤ fruitful rummaging in a vintage or charity store, unearthing another gaspingly gorgeous find to be worn as soon as possible;
- ✤ butterfly kisses, baby Olive in my lap; and,
- ✤ visiting a Parisian café on a mini-break with my husband so we can sit, feet intertwined, sipping coffee, nibbling pistachio macaroons and saying nothing, nothing at all.

I mentioned this to my friend Olivier, who understands and loves fashion as much as I do. *You want to be a fairy,* he said, and I guess that's true. Thirty-three years old and I'm still harbouring fairy fantasies. Oh dear. But fairies don't have a job (apart from flitting about the garden looking pretty). They've no responsibilities, and they're sweet and kind to boot. They don't have to deal with the pesky realities of everyday mundane activities because, naturally, they're not real. Of course I want to be a fairy sometimes. Who wouldn't?

— 4 —

A HOT PINK MOMENT

Like any girl who loves her fashion, I've made too many missteps along the way to remember all of them. But we all remember the first.

In Grade 5—I must have been about ten—I begged my parents to take me to a Blue Light Disco at a nearby school, which they duly did. At this traditional affair, boys plucked girls from chairs lining the walls of the school's gym, aglow in the refracted, coloured light spun from a massive, hired disco ball. I remember being picked by a boy, shorter than me with curly fringe and button nose; dark-collared shirt tucked into high-waisted, acid-wash denim jeans. He led me by the hand to the centre of the sometime basketball court, where we stood a metre apart from each other, shifting from foot to foot and mouthing the words to Starship's 'We Built This City', uncomfortably waiting for it to end.

On my way to centre-stage, I twirled proudly for the sake of my friends; in my home-made bubble skirt, folded-over bobby socks made from hot pink acrylic and a white cotton Wham tee (*Wake Me Up* emblazoned on the front, *Before You Go-Go* on the back), I felt as cool as can be. I loved that shirt—borrowed as it was from my mother at every available opportunity. Almost half a decade off-trend, I cared not a whit and wore it with great hubris, banana clip in my heavily moussed and scrunch-dried hair; illicit frosty pink gloss, stolen from an off-limits bathroom drawer, on my lips.

Even back then, it was all about the outfit. I wasn't sure what all the fuss was about, this boy business. One dressed for their friends, and for the pure pleasure of it—not to please a *boy*. But more on this later.

— 5 —

A RELIGIOUS INTERVENTION
IN THE FORM OF LEGWEAR

In my mid teens, a number of incidents occurred within a short space of time which were the catalyst for a (blessedly short) fashion phase—*la coquette.*

Tracing things back to the first of these incidents I can, in all honesty, say that a pair of opaque tights changed the course of my life.

In my fourteenth year, I was suspended from my all-girls Catholic high school over an altercation with a nun. Not an altercation of the physical kind, but a verbal skirmish over legwear that resulted in my being sent to the principal's office ... before being sent home in shame. I never went back.

Throughout primary and early high school I had attended Catholic colleges. Not because we were much for organised religion, but because private school fees were so high and reports of the misdemeanours committed at our local public schools struck fear into my parents' hearts. So, at twelve, I was packed off to the Marist Sisters' College in Woolwich, in my highly polished Clarks shoes, cotton frock and straw boater, while Jack attended St Mary's, an all-boys school located in the city. He got to wear a sombre dark suit that would not have looked out of place at a funeral. My other brother, Will, was only just starting primary school.

There were aspects of the antiquated, nun-run institution that I enjoyed: the general feeling of bonhomie, the *we're-all-stuck-here-together-so-let's-make-the-most-of-it* interest in extra-curricular activities (which was all very jolly hockey sticks), and the brevity of classes on religious instruction. I was captain of the debating team and a member of the local drama group and that was considered okay, from memory. We attended Home Economics classes, learning to cook and sew to presumably become good little housewives but, in the event this failed, other career options on offer were primary school teaching, nursing or secretarial college (but, then, I wasn't a star student, so it's highly likely these were the paths that students like me were encouraged to take, rather than the only ones on offer).

The summer uniform until Grade 10 was a knee-length cotton-polyester frock with 'loo seat' collar, in a pale blue and white check. Navy blue bias binding edged the aforementioned collar, and the school crest was embroidered on the left breast, beneath which read the Latin phrase *Virtus Super Omnia* (which loosely translates as 'goodness above all'). In winter, the light frock was exchanged for a tunic in itchy navy blue wool, over a long-sleeved blouse with another hideous collar, tie, and ribbed blue tights. It wasn't as bad as the tan and yellow combination of a primary school I'd previously attended, but it was dire nonetheless. The scruffy wags at a nearby public high school would shout at us as our bus went by:

'If dogs could fly, Woolwich would be an airport!'

I blamed the deeply unflattering uniform and would slide down my seat in humiliation for the rest of the journey.

My mother, no doubt preoccupied with her unhappy marriage and the daily grind of looking after three children, did not bat an eyelid when I told her one day that I needed more tights for school, stipulating clearly that could she please buy the opaque—as opposed to ribbed—ones this time? Anyone familiar with wearing a uniform will know (and indeed, any designer will tell you), that when it comes to wearing one well, such very small alterations can change the entire look and feel. A few darts here, a rolled-up cuff there … it's the contrast between one-size-fits-all and couture-like tailoring; the difference between wearing a hessian sack or a chic little number. Opaque tights were my attempt to move one step away from the sack-like qualities of my much-derided school uniform, and one step closer to individuality.

On the day of the opaque tights' virgin outing, I pulled them on with glee and felt the first rumblings of butterflies in my stomach. I walked towards the bus stop, conscious of my newly enhanced pins, and waited patiently for that smoke-belching yellow and maroon bus to roll up. On arriving at school, Emma (first speaker on the debating team) took one look at my legs, raised her left eyebrow and gave me a sly smile, before linking her arm though mine and giving it a little squeeze.

We traipsed down the stone steps to Home Room for morning assembly, where my new tights managed to escape notice … but not for long. As we left the room and headed uphill once again towards our first class in the freezing science labs, I felt a tap on my shoulder and turned to see one of the habit-adorned sisters staring down her long, pointy nose at me, disapproval writ large across her features in the form of downturned mouth and heavily furrowed brow.

'What, may I ask, are you wearing on your legs?'

'Oh, these are just my new tights,' I twittered, a slight stutter revealing my nervousness. 'Mum bought them for me—she must have forgotten they need to be ribbed!'

'Oh, really?' she said, clearly not believing a word of it. 'Well, I shall be calling your mother to come collect you because you can't wear those for the rest of the day. Go!'

Unhappily, I turned away. Thinking her out of earshot, I mumbled 'bitch' in cowardly rebellion under my breath, in an attempt to elicit a laugh from Emma. Not so out of earshot, as it turned out.

'What did I hear you say?' Sister thundered. 'Go see Sister Lamb!' She raised her shaking right arm, pointing ominously towards the principal's office.

So there I was, small and miserable and sitting across from this scary woman I'd had little cause to come into contact with thus far, while she dialled our home number to talk to my mother—no doubt looking forward to the opportunity for both of them to give me a good roasting ...

Despite the fact I was sitting a few feet away, I could still hear my mother's incredulous screech coming through the handset on the desk, once the situation had been explained. To a woman juggling two jobs and three children, being asked to pick me up from school over a pair of tights must have seemed ridiculous. After a heated discussion (in which

I thought Sister Lamb came off second-best), I was sent to wait in the foyer, where I sat dolefully and secretly worked loose threads from the ugly brown upholstered chair while the receptionist answered calls in her dull monotone. I was picked up begrudgingly, without a word, 45 minutes later.

The next few days passed in a blur of arguments between my parents. My mother battled fiercely, and won, which meant I was to be sent off to work in a hairdressing salon rather than returning to school, because: a) the nuns were ridiculous; and, b) I didn't seem to be very good at school anyway. I'd blown my chance for an education, she reasoned. The real world would be all the education I needed.

I appealed to my father with a doleful, hangdog expression and attempts at light conversation, but he refused to talk to me. For the first time, I longed for the frivolity of recess and lunchtime breaks; messing about playing hopscotch and handball with my schoolmates, and dreaming about dances and boys. But I realised I had no choice but to accept my fate.

6

LIFE IN THE FAST LANE

Highlightz was an upmarket North Shore salon for the ladies-who-lunch set. I got a rude shock in my interview (an interview I was strongarmed into attending by my mother, who sat stony-faced beside me, occasionally answering the owner's questions: 'Oh, yes, she has a very strong work ethic'). Thinking my uniformed days well behind me, I was instead presented with a long white linen dress with scoop-neck and fake tortoiseshell buttons down the front. The dress was 1950s American Dairy Queen meets sun frock, which was a hoot as we worked like the proverbial Trojans when we wore them. Leather harnesses and chains would have been more appropriate, but might have given the vanilla clientele a bit of a turn.

But it wasn't all bad. I soon discovered my colleagues were a wild bunch. Not Lorraine, of course, the sunny-faced proprietor with an edge of steel whose greatest thrill was to leave us to it while she counted her substantial day's takings ... but the other apprentices and fully qualified hairdressers who formed my new social set.

There was husky-voiced Mischa, eighteen and in her second year at the local technical college, where I joined her, attending classes as a first-year student. Previously the youngest, Mischa seized upon this opportunity, alternately taking me under her wing and belittling me. She could be quite nasty at times, but I trotted after her like a devoted pet, wholly taken by her worldliness, almond-shaped eyes and trails of corkscrew curls, undercut on one side of her head. Dark and dangerous, Mischa switched salon whites for black fishnets, leather mini-skirts and off-the-shoulder jersey tops when the day was done. She was a 'Like A Virgin'-era Madonna who smoked cigarettes with screen-siren glamour, drove a motorbike and lived for her Friday and Saturday nights. I now knew who I wanted to be when I grew up.

Then there was blonde, baby-faced Jerome, whom I'd initially assumed was gay but who was, in truth, quite the ladies' man. I liked Jerome, with his lean frame and cheeky glint in his eye. He took pity on me and taught me all sorts of things, such as how to give decent head massages, style my hopelessly baby fine hair and spot Mischa's venomous moods in advance. I admired him no end for his ability to charm even the most austere clients, and his tips alone far exceeded my income, which was exactly the minimum wage at just over one hundred dollars a week.

Becca was a platinum blonde of the Anna Nicole Smith variety. Twenty-six, all soft rolling curves and luscious hips constantly straining at white linen seams. Her sticky red lips pouted sexily and I barely saw anything pass them but the small white diet pills she'd developed quite the addiction to.

Dee, older than us all, was a mousy eighties throwback who looked like one of my mother's friends with her shaggy, highlighted 'do, but she partied harder than most and had no intention of 'settling down'. Dee was mostly pleasant and quiet during the day, but after a big night out was to be avoided like the plague.

It was not long before I was initiated into the fold, and smuggled into their favourite Friday night haunts. It was certainly welcome after a gruelling day at the basin, washing toxic colours from clients' heads and sweeping discarded hair into small piles which were then collected into huge garbage bags and deposited in the back lane dumpbins for collection. Jerome worked his magic on my parents, convincing them to let me stay over at Dee's place so we could talk styling techniques and bond over takeaway pizza.

My first night out with this motley crew was a revelation. We did indeed start at Dee's eating pizza but, come 10 pm, off we cabbed to The Exchange, a popular gay bar on Oxford Street. Once there, I careened around the floor, fuelled by a sip from Mischa's vodka tonic, and revelling in Rozalla singing 'Everybody's Free (To Feel Good)'. Life didn't get much better than this, I thought.

That night, I wore a green tie-dyed skirt with ruched waist, hitched up high like a bandeau over barely formed breasts, leaving its hem to fall to mid thigh. I'd paired it with black platform sandals (on loan from Becca). In this outfit, my hands self-consciously wandered to my new bright red crop and fake lashes—expertly applied by Sascha, along with lashings of mascara. I closed my eyes, imagining my fingers on the back of my newly bare neck as not mine but a boy's. Not a dangerous boy's, but those of my opposite number in the Holy Cross College debating team—a bespectacled, geeky type I'd nurtured a crush on, before my debating days were cut short. Debating was the closest I got to encounters with the opposite sex, not counting the de-shirted, shaved and greased gods I partied with beneath The Exchange's glittering, spot-lit podium.

This night at The Exchange paved the way for the year ahead. I realised I adored clubbing in establishments where I barely needed to lie about my age. Gay clubs were notoriously lax on checking IDs, and a safe environment under the circumstances (I had the wrong chromosomes to be of any interest to the regular patrons). The downside was that I developed quite a skewed vision of 'appropriate' attire; this now carried over into my daytime garb, causing my father to order me back to my room to change before leaving the house. Sequinned hotpants and psychedelic patterned tights were a favourite, as were tiny crop tops, cut-off denim shorts and silver fairy dust sprinkled liberally on my cheeks. I must have looked like I'd escaped from a school eisteddfod.

Then the good times ground to an end, as they often do. A regular, Mrs Something-or-other, had been coming to the salon for years to see Dee for the hairstyle *du jour*. At the time, this was a dark red crop with stripey white-blonde highlights. As she sat at the basin, dark red dye slopped all over her hairline, I was charged with removing any traces from her skin before Dee did the blow-dry and sent her on her way, several hundred dollars the poorer. Scrubbing steadily with an astringent solution, I couldn't remove the

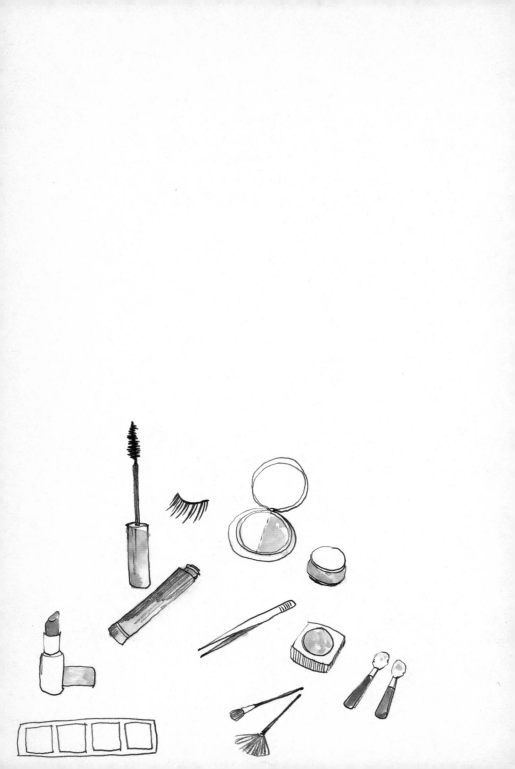

purplish tinge coating the centre of her forehead. Scrubbing like a mad thing and to no avail I cried out, 'Gawd, we'd better get rid of this before you leave—you look like Mikhail Gorbachev!' The salon went suddenly silent. It wasn't colour, as it turns out, but a red-wine stain birthmark she'd been assiduously covering up with a fringe her whole life.

Lorraine led me into the cramped back room where the colourists mixed their foul unguents. A painful 'it's not working out' discussion followed. I saw my dreams of one day owning my own salon, decked out in black and fuchsia, with the cleverly punned name Do or Dye, quickly turn to ash. I put my head in my hands and bawled shamelessly. After which I was sent on my way to trawl the outer suburbs (all the plum, inner-city jobs were gone), searching for another minimum-wage job before they kicked me out of technical college.

With zero luck on this front, I decided to re-enrol in school. On such small moments do our fates turn. But now I attended the local comprehensive with a scary (and justifiably so) reputation. I put my few hairdressing skills to use on my new friends, something which gave me fifteen minutes of fame among the other class mates. That, and my preference for short skirts.

Much of the next few years are hazy in my memory, mixed as they are with feelings of desolation and sadness, for this is the time when I moved out of home and into the spare room of a school friend's family home. My parents' arguments had grown worse, or perhaps I was just more aware of them. Witnessing their altercations made me feel I couldn't breathe. In turn, I know I couldn't have been easy to deal with: dishonest and flouting the not-so-very strict rules they set. On the outside, I kept up a fairly sunny demeanour for those around me; on the inside, I felt broken in two.

To negotiate my way through the finishing of school, I worked a few jobs during the evenings and on weekends, one of which was as a waitress in a local café. In stark contrast to the way I dressed, I was actually a very naïve just-sixteen. Maybe that's why I attracted the attention of Simon, almost twice my age and a café regular, who invited me to his thirtieth birthday party at Saloon, a Wild-West-themed bar. All I know is, I liked the way he looked: jeans, checked shirt and a grease-slicked quiff, which I thought super-cool.

I saw Simon for a month, over which time nothing more serious happened than a peck on the cheek, but by now I was living in my own apartment, shared with a local real estate agent who was barely there for most of the week. Simon and I went out often over that short time, sometimes for dinner or to a bar to see a band, where he gripped my arm tightly and guided me inside (deftly side-stepping any argument from the bouncers whose job it was to check my ID).

Simon liked my outfits—and why wouldn't he? My favourite at the time was a pair of hippie cheesecloth trousers in earthy stripes, low-slung to show off a sun-browned and pierced navel. I'd wear them with a black halter-neck crop top and black leather slip-on boots bearing Cuban heels. I wore this to see a Doors revival band with him, where scantily clad groupies gyrated on stage, worshipping this would-be Jim Morrison as though he were the real thing. And I fashioned my hair in a messy, bleached blonde bob, loosely parted in the middle, and was told I bore more than a passing resemblance to the actress Drew Barrymore, that other little girl lost.

The night I ended it with Simon was the night I made an important decision: no more dressing for men.

The occasion? Dinner with his friends, a couple in their early forties, who lived near the beach. Simon arrived in his boat of an American muscle car to pick me up, and we drove with the top down, barely cooled by the breeze on that midsummer's eve. And my outfit? A short black skirt showing off lots of brown leg. On top, a see-through silk high-neck *chinois* top, embroidered and powdery blue, with a camisole underneath. I could see him studying me, weighing up whether or not I was wearing a bra.

Arriving at his friends' home, we were greeted by an exuberant, curly-haired, spaceman-pyjama-clad toddler, so excited to see Simon (a firm favourite). His mother—a petite, attractive blonde—came smiling into the hall behind him ... and did a double-take on seeing me. An uncomfortable evening ensued, where the woman and her husband—a political cartoonist on a national paper—asked me about school with barely disguised sarcasm, and eyeballed Simon while, I felt, ridiculing me.

As we left I felt tears pricking at my eyes but refused to

cry. I said not a word all the way home, and got out of the car in stony silence. I stopped answering Simon's calls, and soon left my café job where I had cause to run into him. I still can't really articulate the way I felt, but for a long while it seemed everything was so wrong. However, as time passed, I began to feel stronger. I can't pinpoint the change, but the upshot was the gathering of somewhat more self-respect.

—⟶ 7 ⟵—

THE RELEVANCE OF COUTURE

When you are a fashion-obsessed woman of limited means, the concept of haute couture (at least for 99 per cent of the time) remains just that: a concept. But there are some instances where I have rubbed up against, even found myself inside, the genuine article. Not custom-made for me, of course—that would be the real deal—but beautiful items of clothing nonetheless, painstakingly stitched by hand in a design house or by an artisan seamstress for some fabulously wealthy, elegant woman.

I didn't feel any less special being the second recipient of their beauty. Oh, no. They made me feel a million bucks ...

✤ THE RED DRESS ✤

When I was younger, sillier and just out of school, I moved to Melbourne for a boy. The boy promptly upped sticks and left, carving out a large portion of my heart to take with him. I then lived with a varying succession of nuttier and nuttier housemates, until I found myself sharing a tiny *pied-à-terre* in Prahran with Delphi, a contemporary dance student attending the Victorian College of the Arts.

Delphi was mad, but I loved her. We often stayed up until the wee hours having tipsy conversations about the boys we fancied (usually fancying they were nicer boys). Delphi's suggestion, when they inevitably disappointed us, was, *Let's firebomb them!* And we made lists of all those in line for this special treatment, lists that were then tacked with a magnet to the fridge (a fridge which contained nothing more than half a loaf of bread, spreadable butter and a near-empty jar of strawberry jam, along with a bag of ice and bottle of vodka in the freezer). Initially, I thought she was joking, but when I got to know her better it did seem a tactic Delphi would willingly have employed should romantic negotiations go sour.

So there we were, bemoaning the absence of eligible men and wondering what was wrong with us. I had developed terrible acne that I tried to cover up with layers of pore-clogging foundation, and was altogether too blonde and cheery for the moody Melbourne climate. Delphi was the opposite, and had a touch of the saucy burlesque dancer about her with her porcelain skin, dark curls and elegantly arched brows—and a brashness that may have had something to do with the gender-bending crowd she mixed with. Looking back, I think the tortured, arty men I met during this period thought I was more akin to a Labrador puppy trailing around after them than a serious love interest. And they were simply dead scared of Delphi.

My friend Rodney—dear Rodney of the blonde sideburns, coiff and razor-sharp wit—insisted on naming me after a cocktail: the Fluffy Duck. That might give you an indication of how seriously I was taken because, of course,

they were all years and years older than me, those boy-men I
pined for. I was particularly enamoured of Rodney because
he showered me with semi-compliments: 'You're a sword
wrapped in a silk sheath' or 'You're an enigma wrapped in a
mystery' ... which made me feel all clever and desirable and
kept me eager to hear more.

During this time, my wardrobe changed frequently as I
tried on different attitudes for style. My hair morphed every
six weeks—from platinum curls to a half-blonde-half-black
Debbie Harry 'do, from red stripes to a bleached crop—
thanks to my patronage of a local hairdresser who went by
the name of Fur.

One day, I was flicking through the frocks in my closet,
searching for something spectacular to wear on a date with
a beautiful half-Japanese musician, whose perfect oval
face was peppered with freckles. I fancied he looked like a
Benetton model. Delphi came to my room wearing a silk
slip, cocktail in hand, and leant against the door frame in
a sultry imitation of Liz Taylor in *Who's Afraid of Virginia Woolf?*
(we were always emulating old films back then just to inject
a little glamour into life).

'What's up, dear one?' she asked.

I wailed about my predicament—all my frocks were *wrong,*
wrong, wrong—and Delphi snapped her fingers.

'Alors! Come into my boudoir.'

She wasn't exaggerating—Delphi really did have a
boudoir. Her queen-sized bed (a futon—we all had one back
then) was covered in a shimmering velvet eiderdown of deep
red. Her bedside lamps were draped in silk scarves, casting
an atmospheric glow on the walls—dark fringing all the

better for creating moody, dappled shadows. My room may have had the built-in wardrobe, but Delphi's contained one long, industrial sweatshop-sized rack boasting her impressive collection of floaty kaftans, sixties mini-dresses, men's tuxedos and silk slips in shades of chartreuse, aubergine and maroon. Many more delectable items were heaped in little middens around the room, discarded. Delphi was never one for tidiness—the perfect foil to my near-OCD ordering.

She snapped through the hanging selection, dismissing one after the other, before pushing back the hangers to dramatically present a spectacular, tomato-red silk dress, dusted with tiny silver beads that caught the light. A star dancer who Delphi had met had given it to her in a fit of generosity. It had been bespoke-made for the star by a famed Italian dressmaker, for a European production of *Carmen*.

'Try it on,' coaxed Delphi.

This dress had me in raptures. Its draped, hand-stitched bodice and thin spaghetti straps fell to layered wisps of barely there silk, wisps which floated over thighs and cascaded flatteringly to the knee and trailed away at the back to a point.

'Are you sure?' I cagily enquired (I had no intention of relinquishing it)—as Delphi nodded her assent.

'Uh-huh. I won't be needing it anytime soon,' she said.

It was early summer, so I paired that lovely dress with strappy bronze sandals and a vintage silk fringed shawl picked out with small embroidered roses. I gathered my pre-crop hair into a messy upsweep, curling heavy bangs with a brush to frame my face. The look I was going for was part Marianne Faithfull, part gypsy Russian ballet dancer. A small burgundy velvet clutch completed the look. I was ready.

Oh, that frock was beautiful. I felt like a princess from a Hans Christian Andersen fairytale, stepping out to meet her prince. It was only mine for the evening (Delphi was a hoarder—she didn't give anything away), but I found excuses to sashay proudly up and down Greville Street a few times, attracting what I felt to be the most admiring glances I'd received in my entire time in Melbourne.

What do they say about pride coming before a fall?

My date never did turn up that night, leaving me stranded in a local restaurant, feeling more foolish as the seconds ticked by. Some friends came in half an hour later, spied me looking forlorn in a corner booth—I hadn't even thought to bring a paperback for company—and invited me to join them. We had a meal of roasted globe artichokes covered with *salsa verde* for dinner, then we moved on to a darkened bar where I drowned my sorrows in a forgotten number of bottles of red wine, before teetering home around 2 am, alone.

This was in the days before everybody had mobile phones. I received a call to my landline the next day; something about a forgotten gig and no way of getting hold of me, *blah blah blah* (my last brief encounter with a musician—I washed my hands of them from that day forth). I was forgiving, but firm. There would be no second chance to see me in that red dress.

Despite (or maybe because of) the drama, I remember it fondly, that gorgeous frock, tied up as it is with memories of Delphi and being so young and unlucky in love.

✤ THE BLACK GIVENCHY ✤

A number of years later, in London, I shared a home with a lovely family of three. Patricia, John and five-year-old Arabella Winham were renovating their 1930s Wandsworth cottage, and had a spare room they wanted to rent out for some extra cash. Enter: me.

I was out almost every night, and for most of the weekend and, of course, worked every weekday—so I made the ideal boarder. I was home only for Sunday lunch, when Trisha made a gorgeous roast chicken with rosemary potatoes and I sat on the large flagstones of the kitchen floor, playing with Arabella and admiring her dwarf bunnies. Arabella let me stroke their silky coats while she muttered sweet nothings in their ears, and occasionally let me feed one a rubbery stub of carrot or wilted lettuce leaf.

That home was full of love, light and so much happiness. It showed me where I wanted to be in a decade's time.

A couple of months before moving in with the Winhams, I had met James (drumroll), my future husband. We were living *la vida loca*, going out every night for dinner and dancing and gathering vast groups of friends together in an attempt to share the love. It was such a happy time. But given that I worked in the notoriously badly paid publishing industry, and my rent and living expenses in that costly city were substantial, my outgoings far exceeded my meagre incomings. Before long I found myself in serious debt, which was when I decided to move out of the lovely Clapham South terrace I'd been sharing with two far-better-remunerated friends, and in with the Winhams. I also left my book publishing job to take up a position as publicity manager at a major British recruitment firm.

One night I was preparing to go out for a high-profile work event I'd organised, my first—an annual ball for hundreds of plum clients at a swanky Park Lane hotel. I'd arranged everything myself, from the items on the menu to the guest speaker and evening's schedule. A lot of responsibility was resting on my shoulders—blowing it was not an option.

That night, none of the outfits I tried seemed right for that upmarket venue. I'd already felt out of place there when attending mid-week meetings to finalise the arrangements … and this was a Saturday night, with everyone dressed to the nines. My head hurt thinking about it, so I gave up and decided to take a bath. Divine inspiration might come to me there. On my way upstairs I ran into Trisha, who asked me what I'd decided to wear. She must have noted the pained expression on my face, because she smiled and silently led me into her bedroom and towards her over-flowing wardrobe. She pulled down a vacuum-packed bag from the top shelf.

'These are all the things I can't bear to throw out, even though they don't fit me any more, and I can't imagine ever wearing them again. I'm saving them for Arabella.'

At forty-one, Trisha had a lovely figure, but was not as lithe as she'd once been. The family breadwinner, she was a successful architect who worked for herself out of her home office, but back in her twenties she'd been a shop assistant in West London's chic Ladbroke Grove. That's where she'd obtained all the luscious specimens now laid out on the queen-sized bed before me.

I carefully pawed through silk jersey and wool in the most delicately rendered colours imaginable: pale pink, honey nougat, buttery pistachio, spicy tomato and a lovely cornflower blue. But my hands came to rest on a little black number, and wrested it from the pile. The shoulder straps were of twisted silk, very Grecian in style, which fell to a draped bodice and bias-cut skirt. Perfect for the cocktail dress code which I'd set myself.

'Oh, you'll love that. Go on, try it,' Trisha urged.

I stripped down to my undergarments and slipped the diaphanous sheath over my head, pulling it gently over waist and hips while it settled into place. Trisha gave a little gasp and spun me around to face the mirror. I couldn't believe it—it fit like the proverbial glove.

'You have to wear it—it looks as though it was made for you,' Trisha said.

Trisha told me the story of that dress. It was from a fashion PR showroom she'd once been invited to attend. When she'd admired it on a rack in the corner of the room, the rep had said, *Oh, that—you can have it. It's a sample and it's got a ciggie burn in the side anyway*—and promptly flung it at her to take.

That dress, sample though it was, and despite the cigarette burn, which Trisha had had craftily mended, bore the design house's name: Givenchy. Years before it had swished its way down the catwalk. I know, because I later saw a picture of it in a runway report in a back issue of UK *Vogue*. In contrast with the glitz and glamour of the heavily embellished gowns in that showroom, this black number would have seemed plain in the extreme, yet its design pedigree was unmissable: the cut was impeccable, and so flattering I felt as though I never wanted to take it off.

I wore Trisha's dress that night with my hair fashioned into a simple French roll as a nod to Hubert de Givenchy's home country. My feet shod in high black stilettos, my outfit needed no more decoration than the single gold cuff I clipped on my wrist. Standing at the venue's door next to my uptight manager, helping him greet people as they arrived, I felt drugged with confidence. No matter that later on, the well-known comedian I'd carefully chosen as a speaker took offence to bawdy heckling from the crowd and tipped a glass of ale on a CEO's head, causing a minor furore. Or that the first course (an ill-chosen soup) came out uniformly tepid, even though it wasn't gazpacho. And if that were not enough, with the night falling on the same date as a World Cup football match, we also lost the attention of the entire male contingent as they scurried to watch it being televised. The event was bordering on being *un catastrophe,* and my manager scowled at me for the duration of it. But such is the power of a good dress—I felt invincible. Afterwards, I met some friends to go out dancing in the West End until the wee hours, tip-toeing home at first light with stilettos in hand, feet torn to shreds.

Anything that gives you the confidence to walk into a room knowing you look your very best is a rare thing. It's a thrill I'd wish on any woman at least once in her life. You don't need couture to pull it off ... but it certainly helps.

——⟊ 8 ⟊——

WHERE HAVE YOU BEEN ALL MY LIFE?

There are clothes I have yearned for my whole life. Clothes that I subconsciously search for in every fashionable store I walk into. These are the items that I know will perfectly articulate my personality, or at least a certain facet of it, come the right situation. But they always seem to be just out of my reach.

✤ NUMBER ONE ✤

A perfectly cut, Breton-style top. Made of heavyweight cotton the shade of clotted cream, it has thin (but not too thin) navy blue stripes, travelling horizontally. The traditional boat neck sits high, but just loose enough to expose elegantly jutting clavicles which I'm not sure I even possess, and the fit is generous but skims my shape in all the right places, hinting at a spare leanness beneath—because good clothes can do that, even without the requisite body. Or at least make a less-than-ideal body appear desirable.

My inspiration? Pablo Picasso in a Robert Doisneau photograph taken in 1952, titled *Picasso and the Loaves,* where Pablo is wearing my top, arms placed on the table in front of him and bulbous fingers of bread posed in place of his hands. In my mind, this is an image juxtaposed with the French actress Audrey Tautou in the film *Coco Avant Chanel*.

Picasso and Audrey want me to have Breton success. They whisper over my shoulder every time I conduct an online search, or flick through the racks of yet another collection of clothes for the new season. They urge me to keep trying. *Don't give up*, they say encouragingly. *N'abandonne pas. Never fear*, I respond. *I won't.*

Precisely what am I trying to say? *So Frenchy, so chic … I have a European sensibility, harking back to those intercontinental jetsetters of the 1950s, don't you know?* The kind of woman you would find, hands planted on hips, at the prow of a yacht which skips towards the crest of yet another wave. The kind of woman who blasts you with a 100-watt smile. Set curls and a mostly all-white outfit, denying the existence of small jammy fingers and dirt of any kind. Voluptuous red lips; Russian red, with a hint of frosty blue. Not a care in the rarefied world.

A kindly colleague once gifted me a long Jean Paul Gaultier dress in the Breton style, with gothic pewter buttons along the shoulder blades. I thought I'd found my Breton fix. I wore it out to dinner one night with three girlfriends; nails painted black, hair pulled tight in a high ponytail, metal crosses swinging from my ears and feet in Roman sandals. We picked at sushi and gossiped about work. Pretty much

Breton
(with
black
leather
jacket)

your standard girlie catch-up, with all of us dressed with subtle precision in a way that only other women and certain men pick up on. Their outfit approval gave me an inner glow.

But I was freed from its charms not long after, with the realisation that it was far too long, and too high. The buttons made me claustrophobic—I longed to release the aforementioned clavicles. I considered cutting it short, but Jean Paul chided me as I brandished my big black-handled dressmaking scissors, and I lost my nerve. I passed it on to a friend, but can't remember now to whom exactly.

At least the Breton is a classic. Designers grand and not-so-grand bring out new versions every season, so I might actually find it one day. Case in point: French Connection has a decent Breton-style dress this year, purchased by a friend of mine, and British designer Margaret Howell rocked Breton out in tops on the catwalk a few seasons ago. But by the time I saw the images there was nary a one to be found anywhere.

✤ NUMBER TWO ✤

A super-flattering bodysuit that sculpts the form and doesn't fall apart after two washes. To be worn layered under a billowing see-through dress, or wrap skirt, or a pair of jeans and blazer with high heels.

I'm getting very tired of bodysuits that go all ball-y and horrible after one wash. Even worse, when the fabric distorts like a swimming costume you've worn one too many times. Good bodysuits are hard to find. I mean, *really* hard. I have several, and they're all disappointing in one way or another.

I read somewhere that Wolford offer the best on the market. Do they really last forever, given the right care? I can hardly believe it. Time to start saving, if they do.

✤ NUMBER THREE ✤

A timeless LBD (Little Black Dress, for the uninitiated). An amazing LBD is the stuff of legend. I have several black dresses that almost fit the bill—five, to be precise—but none of them is *the* LBD.

The LBD is the frock you throw on to give you confidence when you're feeling rushed for time, washed out, nervous, or hormonal and incapable of making a wise decision. It's the dress to wear to an important business meeting under a blazer or smart cardigan, to a chic cocktail party with killer heels, to dinner with new people, or on a first date. It's the one item of clothing every woman should possess. The frock you can count on when all else fails ... and that's why I know I definitely don't own it (yet).

To be honest, it doesn't even need to be black. Maybe it's midnight blue, or deep plum. Something monochromatic and slimming, cut like a dream, and made of a fabric that calms you, as opposed to setting the teeth on edge.

My black dresses are lovely, to be sure, but let me explain why none of them is *the* LBD:

Black dress A: the ex-debutante
I have a 1950s floor-length gown, made of a very heavy fabric and boned to sculpt the top half of the body in a perfect hourglass shape. It's adorned with only a thin strip of ivory-coloured broderie anglaise stitched across the top of the bodice, and was worth every penny at fifty bucks from a flea market. The previous owner purchased it online from a vintage supplier in the US, and took out the original pockets (it's something I'm sad about, but I haven't yet tried putting new ones back in).

My gown looks amazing with a chignon and large round bangle, and is perfect for parties, certain lunches (with a bright, white cotton shirt knotted over the top, strappy silver sandals peeking out from beneath its draped lengths) and for seriously swishy occasions, but is inappropriate for almost anything else.

Black dress B: the flirt
This is a sexy little lace slip of a thing, to be worn over a silk shift. This dress is the ticket for cocktails and dinner, but otherwise too insubstantial and a bit tarty—especially under

bright lights, where it reveals every single bump and curve, and a slightly over-enthusiastic cleavage.

I love that frock, and given the above she actually falls to rather a modest length, just below the knees. But she's like the boyfriend you don't want to introduce to everybody, lest they judge you incorrectly; ever so slightly 'not me'.

Black dress C: the retro queen
Another heavy, slightly stretchy knee-length number, tulip-shaped, with spaghetti straps and a tightly fitted bodice. It looked magic at the thirtieth birthday party I attended once in the grounds of some stately country pile in Yorkshire. Then, I wore it with towering peep-toe pumps in burnished gold and ornate faux-emerald-encrusted drop earrings.

This little beauty is heaven worn over a red and white striped top, paired with metallic ballet slippers. But its tulip shape falls in and out of favour, so much so that I have often considered getting rid of it, but instead store it away in tissue paper each season it's on the out, until I'm ready to face it again with fresh eyes. One day she'll be back, so my devotion to her is on hold until then.

Black dress D: subtle chic
She's an understated beauty ... a sumptuous silk velvet shift with scalloped hem. Sleeveless and a little 1920s in design, falling directly from chest to mid-thigh with no discernible shape in between. I thought she might be *the one,* but while the shapelessness is good for days when I'm feeling, shall we say, overindulged, it's no good when you want to make a splash. She's tasteful, but a bit too much so for my liking.

I've taken to wearing her during the day when I've nothing special planned, with fitted cardigan or ornate Dries Van Noten or Indian-style ethnic vest with inset mirrors over the top, and some longish beads. That alone tells me she's no LBD; saved for special occasions, or when in dire need (in emergencies, break glass).

Black dress E: the kook
Almost, almost there ... but yet so far. This is a cheeky little eighties number that represents the best of the era: the top half's made from a thick, stretchy material, a bit scuba in flavour, cut singlet-style and low in the back, it hugs the frame like a bodysuit. The bottom half? A gloriously frothy, netted skirt dotted with small gold discs. It's quite short and quite low-cut, but the full skirt gives it girlish charm (in short, she's no tart). Inside it I feel like a trapeze artist escaping from the circus for the day; the love interest in film-maker Wim Wenders' wonderful film, *Wings of Desire*. Why is she not right? Well, one can't be a trapeze artist all the time, I'm afraid.

My point is, it's very difficult for one item of clothing (in this case, a little black dress) to fulfil all your needs. It's a great deal of responsibility to rest on the shoulders of one insubstantial slip of fabric. Between them, my five dresses cover most bases, but in the interests of paring back and spending less time standing in front of my wardrobe, perennially despairing that I have nothing to wear, I'd like my choices to be a little simpler. When it

ex - debutante

the flirt

the retro queen

comes to alighting upon the perfect dress for all occasions, no choice at all would (almost) be better.

So my search for the LBD has stalled for a bit. Ironically, I think I've actually found it, but I'm not prepared to invest in it—just yet—for the potential LBD I've earmarked is an asymmetrical Vivienne Westwood number, costing the heady price of a month's mortgage instalment. Made of thick, stretchy jersey (good for sucking in, in all the right places), it saucily hugs the curves to mid-calf. Boning and corsetry push the breasts up and out: *un peau* serving-wench, but tasteful. The cut's unique and recognisable, and each drape and detail is enough to incite in me roiling thrills of rapture. She currently resides on my Net-A-Porter wish list.

the
Kook

subtle chic

I've encouraged friends to buy it, even though it feels like that dress has my name on it. Perhaps I want to keep it close, live vicariously through them. Like a potential lover you know you must not have; the one you set up on a date with your best friend because you really want him for yourself …

And while I'm all for spending a mortgage payment irresponsibly once in a while, I need to be able to justify it, at least to myself, even in a nonsensical way. Cost-per-wear calculations, and all that rubbish.

This LBD would sit on my sizeable clothes rack waiting for just one of the many occasions I mentioned above, but they don't come around so very often nowadays, given that I'm the mother of a small child, and mostly at home, and mostly attending morning or afternoon teas, and lazy lunches, the supermarket and market stalls. I do attend special dinners, and last-minute events, but they are so rare right now as to be negligible in making this special purchase worth it. And I'm not daft enough to expect it'll still be *the one* in five years' time. Not even an LBD is capable of that.

B ut what is the worst feeling? To find the frock, or the top, or the cigarette-legged trousers—and fall shamelessly, head over heels in love. To sense this very piece is exactly what you've been searching for all this time: a rare gem that suits you to a T. Only to then glance upon the price tag, feel your heart skip a beat before sinking like a stone to your stomach, and know unequivocally, *not today.* Maybe not ever. You sadly return it to the rack, heart cleaved in half. A piece of you is missing.

I had that sinking feeling once during a shopping jaunt with my fabulously successful friend Patti, the CFO of a major company. I spied a pair of wide-legged Chloé jeans in Harrods while she was trying on a Prada frock. (I know, why torture myself? A shopping 'spree' when someone else does the spending—even a beloved friend—when you've no purchasing power of your own, is no real fun at all. It's the same as being at a spectacular sale when all they have left are size 8s, and you're a size 12.)

Anyway, I digress ...

Chambray blue, with red piping around the pockets and shiny scarlet buttons, I've almost deified those jeans in my head. The podium they were displayed on, lit from below by soft beams, only enhanced the heaven-sent impression. And although I'm aware of the wily marketing technique employed against me, I haven't stopped worshipping my false idol. If only I owned those jeans, life would be better, brighter, more fun. And I'd be braver along with it. They'd go with every single top in my wardrobe. Don't tell me I'm wrong; I know it to be true.

But far worse is the one that got away, and knowing you just let it slip through your fingers.

There was the time my husband and I attended a music festival in late summer. As is common at such events, there were a few clothing stalls selling rack upon rack of quite good-quality vintage pieces, which we browsed in the lull between bands. I tried on a little grey cashmere cardigan, the colour of the sea when it reflects the winter sky. Covered in elegant pewter beading, and fastened by pearl buttons with a distinctly petrol-ish sheen, she was lined with the finest silk, sewn in by hand by someone very patient.

The day was steamy. No sooner had I tried on that woolly number than I whipped it off, feeling scratchy-hot already. It hardly went with the denim cut-offs, studded sandals and long, loose-flowing tank I was wearing. I contemplated it, head slightly fuzzy from the heat and one downed can of warmish lemonade and Stolichnaya vodka.

'Nah, too granny,' James declared over his shoulder, flicking through the racks.

'Really? I think I like it,' I said. 'It's only thirty bucks.'

Unsure, I reluctantly replaced it on the padded coat-hanger and returned it to the rack, my hand still rested on its sleeve. Then, an olive-skinned, raven-haired beauty with almond eyes shoved me slightly in her haste to grab that cardigan. James and I turned around as one, to see her preening in front of the mirror. I watched her pinch off, between thumb and forefinger, one of the pearly petrol buttons that had been hanging by a thread.

'Can I have it for twenty-five?' she called out to the stallholder. 'The button fell off!'

'Sure,' he replied.

Seconds later she was gone. James raised his eyebrows, while I cursed him under my breath.

I cannot tell you how many times I have thought of that cardigan. Each time I'm standing in front of a full-length mirror—in a chosen frock or my current favourite pair of jeans, flinging on fur gilet after blazer after scarf to find the right look for a night out that might turn chilly—I long for that cardigan. She would have gone with this, and that, and this, I think. That lost little number seems now to have been the answer to all my sartorial prayers. I hope the Raven is enjoying her. James has heard me bang on about it more than once, but he has the good grace not to remind me that it was *myself* who faltered in the decision to buy it.

I've just about forgiven him.

At the risk of sounding ridiculous, here's my advice, my little secret: carry around, in your diary or purse, a list of the items you're looking for, to be referred to in times of need. Just in case you forget, or waver. The list also works as a mantra, drawing good things in.

Try it—I swear it will make shopping easier. Well, at least some of the time.

9

COSTUMES NOUVEAUX

Travel is an experience which changes our perspective on everything and, in particular, any preconceived notions we have about fashion. It's changed my own sense of style immeasurably, and has been most responsible for the development of my somewhat eccentric, chameleon tastes, because I have always wanted to adapt to each new environment I've found myself in.

I love being mistaken for a local wherever I go. My idiocy with languages means that as soon as I open my mouth the gig's up, but it's a thrill pretending to be someone else in the interim. Only here, at home, do I throw all those influences together to bring a little France, or a little London, or a little Brazil into my world each day, in constantly evolving fits of eclectic whimsy. Everywhere else, I can't help it: I always travel with a theme.

My overseas jaunts have also made me realise that the only universal aspect of fashion is the passion so many of us have for it; the very human instinct for change, and the innate drive to look our best. What's positively outré in one place is old news somewhere else, and certain things will never be 'got' in different climates or timezones.

For example, wearing head-to-toe black in some parts of Europe will have you mistaken for a widow; and try dressing down in a pair of Havaianas thongs when far from a beach ... But an appreciation of fashion is a thread stitched into the DNA of every place I've ever visited, and there is always something, or someone, to catch and amuse the eye.

Growing up on a diet of novels and foreign magazines, and nurturing a pretension for arty independent films as a teenager, I thought I knew a bit about what people wore overseas. But it never felt enough to simply study the world through a page or a screen; I desperately longed to live *inside* it. Travelling was always on the agenda, and I felt it would change me, for the good.

The first place I visited in Asia was a two-week stop-over in Thailand, on the way to start a new life in Hong Kong. Having only previously travelled to (what I felt to be safe) European countries, I read up on what to expect, perhaps focusing a little too heavily on tales of food poisoning, murder and organ thieves.

Flying into Bangkok with my then-boyfriend Tom, our first step out onto the tarmac was almost indescribable, assailed as we were with a dense, wet heat, the smell of human perspiration and something spicy, with an undercurrent of rotting food. The chopped-up durian fruit we'd been warned about, sold by street hawkers just outside their doors, gave off more than a slight whiff of puke. Clothes felt instantly redundant; I could have literally ripped off the black synthetic sheath I'd worn on the plane, in my eagerness to find some relief from the sticky heat.

Already feeling shell-shocked by all the touts who descended on us as one, we chose a taxi and kept our fingers firmly crossed (to be safe). First stop: the hotel, recommended by Lonely Planet, down the end of a long street lined with savagely broken cement blocks and empty building sites, sniffed at by scruffy looking dogs with ribs visible beneath mange-covered skin. Los Angeles, following the riots, came to mind. And, at a pinch, war-torn Bosnia. After the death-defying trip down the highway, suicidally weaving our way through traffic and narrowly avoiding the city's heaving populace (I covered my eyes as we navigated through it, certain we were about to collide with a *tuk tuk*, bus, people, or all three), all of a sudden, here in this street, there was no-one to be seen. I suspected the taxi driver was kidnapping us—we'd be robbed of all our possessions, chopped up into little pieces and never heard from again.

But just as I prepared myself to scream, here he was stopping outside a building, a recognisable name emblazoned across its crumbling façade. Our hotel. We paid and thanked him with barely disguised relief. Inside the hotel, our eyes took some time to adjust to the darkened interior, gilded ceiling fans lazily circling above us. Two winding staircases of cool grey marble descended to the floor, comfy brown leather armchairs arranged in a semi-circle at their feet. A man in chinos and a Panama hat reclined, reading a paper with English headlines; a battered tan satchel sat at his side on the cool shiny floor. I was reminded of Hemingway, and Graham Greene.

A beautiful, petite woman with a glossy black ponytail, wearing a long skirt suit of tropical hues, appeared at my elbow and offered us cool drinks of fresh fruit, the glass beaded with moisture, just like me. I declined, noting the ice cubes. I'd read about those—likely to have you throwing up for a week. After checking in we headed up to our room, me regretting my rejection of that drink more and more with every step.

Despite the promising look of the lobby, our room was very basic, a working air-conditioning unit the only thing to recommend it. But who cared? It encouraged us to go out all day and night, exploring the city by foot, train and in cabs whenever we grew too weary, weaving our way through night markets after dining on river prawns, chicken and pomelo salad, curries infused with coconut, chillies and a trove of spices we could barely recognise—and each more rapturously received than the last.

I bought pyjamas, handmade to fit, in burgundy and gold, and gold and turquoise; little camisoles and short shorts in shiny satin, and a longer pair for cold nights, to be worn in many months' time, from a tailor's shop near Siam Square. Zesty raw silk scarves—quite thin—in aqua, pink and lime green from Jim Thompson's House (the famous American silk importer who'd gone missing in mysterious circumstances in 1967). They could zhoosh up any plain outfit and be worn around the neck, the waist, the wrist or banded about the head. I still have the pink one from that first trip, the only one that is not shredded from over-use.

Following the advice of a kindly local man we found ourselves outside a *wat* (temple)—after paying a gnarled woman to release a clutch of small, twittering birds from a cage for the benefit of our souls. I had my first trouser suit made, from a fine, dark Italian wool. As reference, I clutched a picture of Christy Turlington modelling a favoured style: pleated darts at the trousers' high waist, the pants billowed at the thighs and tapered to a thin ankle; a loose waistcoat, lined with a golden mango silk; and a matching three-button blazer with padded shoulders, falling to mid-thigh, to be worn with a white shirt, tails out. The style was well on its way to being out of date, but I thought it somehow classic—I'd been holding onto that picture for years. I wore it exactly once, because it never quite properly fit.

After three days in Bangkok, we journeyed down to the coast, taking a boat on dangerously rough seas towards Phi Phi Island, where we stayed in a wooden hut on a mountain overlooking the beach. Our days were spent scuba diving, kayaking, swimming and eating, this last in any one of the town's many open-air bars and restaurants.

I discarded the simple separates I had packed—loose shifts, fitted tank tops, Bermuda shorts and plain skirts—in favour of the cheap, bright pieces I acquired at street stalls and at large markets such as Chatuchak—a covered market so huge, it seemed to take up an entire suburb. My cotton and linen separates, in neutral tones of white, navy and beige, matched with one chunky red bangle (the only jewellery I had brought), had looked so chic and French when I had laid them out on the bed back home—my take on Riviera-style holiday dressing when I was so unsure what to expect. Now, these clothes felt too formal for the environs,

teeming with colour and life as it was. And they seemed somehow redundant when we were doing so much active exploring, rather than reclining by the beach. It became a case of adapting on the run. Thai fisherman's pants, earthy batik wraparound skirts and flowy singlets became the staples of my new theme, Miss Khaosan Road (that famous tourist street, immortalised by Alex Garland's novel *The Beach*), matched perfectly with tan leather sandals I already owned. And beads: I bought strings and strings of them. Made from wood and shell and tarnished, beaten metal— I adored their 'thrown on' charm, winding them around neck, arms and ankles ... maybe going a little overboard.

My clothes, more relaxed by the day, reflected my comfort in settling into the equatorial environment. I quickly noted the absence of thuggish gangs lurking on every corner, waiting for us to approach so they could strike. I became fascinated by the religion and customs, and in no time grew to adore the craziness of the driving, the friendliness of the beautiful Thai people and, above all, the food. But I still remained wary, refusing to eat at the less salubrious-looking street stalls, and always cleaning my hands with antibacterial wipes when I did. I checked newly purchased bottles of water to make sure the seal had not been broken (apparently empties were sometimes filled with unfiltered water, but this could have been an urban myth), and drank ice-cold beer instead of mixed spirits (avoiding those ice cubes!). Tom had no such qualms, wolfing down all sorts of things containing mystery meat, and scoffed at my prissiness with the water and wipes. You can guess what happened next.

The final few days of our holiday ended on a low note, with me having to take Tom to the hospital to be attached to an IV—the poor thing had eaten something which made him violently ill, and he spent our remaining 48 hours in Thailand very sick indeed. While he recuperated, I went shopping nearby, jamming my already overflowing bag with trinkets and miniature Buddhas for friends back home. And scarves, a little stack of them, to offer up as treats.

When I collected Tom from the hospital we were given an IV on a wheelie thing to take with us on the plane, and we were seated in business class. We smiled at each other, quite excited by the preferential treatment, and mimed pinching ourselves at our luck—despite the fact he was so weak.

Another trip I remember vividly was my first time to New York, with wardrobe inspired by the ladies of *Friends*. It was June 2001, I was twenty-four, and Rudolph Giuliani was Mayor. The city was brash and fabulous, which I was expecting, but also friendly and pretty, which I'm fairly certain I was not. Landmark destinations, Central Park and the Chrysler Building, were more awe-inspiring than I'd hoped. And SoHo—art and fashion central—blew my mind. But then, I was lucky enough to see New York from a very favourable position: tagging along with Tom while he was on a business trip. I took advantage of the free accommodation in his upmarket hotel suite on midtown Madison Avenue, not far from the park, and happily immersed myself in New York City life for two whole weeks—virtually by myself—while he worked like a mad thing around the clock, and I blew all my hard-earned savings from working in Hong Kong.

The whirlwind began with the speedy cab ride from JFK, our heads swivelling to take in the view from the grubby back windows. I thought of how much I longed to be mistaken for a native in New York, the world's most quintessential city.

We checked in to our hotel, admiring the marble surfaces and understated opulence of the lobby, and left our suitcases for the bell boy to bring up. Given the lack of view from our sixth floor room, I switched on the huge television and saw an ad for jazz pianist and crooner Diana Krall, a personal favourite, who was playing not far from us that very evening. Jetlag forgotten, I did a little happy dance around the room, halting only for the bell boy's knock on the door. Suitcases opened and unpacked mere minutes later, I became thoroughly occupied by the cacophony of thoughts in my head which revolved around only two things: *Where to go first ... and what to wear?*

Opting for a fitted, pale blue cotton-silk midriff top with tiny mother-of-pearl buttons down the front, and my favourite pair of straight leg indigo jeans, plus a long silk scarf wrapped around my bob-exposed neck, I could just see myself in my mind's eye as a modern-day Isadora Duncan. I would sail down the street gracefully, scarf flowing in the wind behind me, leaving a trail of people in my wake thinking, *Who's that girl?* My vanity has never served me well when I'm on holiday.

I agonised over the shoes to match with this smart-casual ensemble, considering my options; from a pair of Roman sandals to trainers and heels. The kitten-heel mules easily won out over the sensible, springy cross trainers (which had safely carried me for miles on a treadmill); and I was definitely aiming for more smart New Yorker than my bronze hippie sandals could deliver. The heels, in a fetching faux-pony-skin zebra print, were box-fresh. I might be a tourist (and I had every intention of exploring the city on foot), but *dammit,* I didn't want to look like one.

It was 8 am on the day we arrived when I kissed my boyfriend goodbye on glitzy Madison Avenue and boldly teetered off in the direction of downtown, voluminous leather bag with chain straps tucked under my right arm, and camera safely hidden. I don't do backpacks—it's part of my whole looking-like-a-local thing—and I've always shuddered on seeing people wearing a camera slung about their necks. *Quelle* ridiculous! You wouldn't catch me dead snapping away in plain view (which is why I have so few pictures from my travels ... and, yes, I've regretted it ever since).

Less than a block later, I felt the first signs of a rapidly forming blister ... I needed to get some breakfast anyway. Popping into a small hole-in-the-wall diner with large plate-glass window and bench, I perched myself precariously atop a stool to watch the street traffic and ordered granola and coffee. The first was delicious, while the latter made me gag. Sitting there in that window for the better part of an hour, I studied men marching by in finely tailored suits with briefcases, and striking women, also suited, striding out in killer heels to conquer the day—while a cloud of steam atmospherically rose from a metal lid bolted to the ground across the street, just like it does in the movies. My first impression of these native New Yorkers was all glossy, blow-dried hair and blindingly white, professionally straightened teeth. New York is a very good-looking city. I pondered on New York, Darwin and his theories on evolution. If this was the most important city in the world, and a favoured destination for every single person I knew, surely I was witnessing the very top of the human food chain.

Eventually my granola was finished and the peak-hour traffic had thinned out so, coffee barely touched, I ventured out once again. It was not long before I was in agony. Oh, dear. I bravely limped on until the first shoe shop I saw, where I ducked in and bought the least ugly pair of trainers I could find. By that stage I had not one, but several angry-looking blisters. Just a glance at my poor battered feet made me feel queasy. I swallowed a few painkillers, wrapped my feet in bandaids kindly supplied by the sales assistants, donned a thick pair of new socks and the shoes, before setting out again. It was a far humbler little mouse that continued on in that big city, vanity firmly in check.

It wasn't all blisters, however. New York was to be positively blissful.

For the following two weeks, I adopted an indulgent routine. I left the hotel with Tom in the morning, bought a toasted bagel with cream cheese from a favourite local bakery, and coffee from Starbucks (bland, but reassuringly predictable), then walked uptown to the park, sat on a bench in the sunshine and watched New Yorkers pass by. Sometimes I read my book (Henry James's moody, beautiful *The Wings of the Dove*; a strange choice in that steamy urban environment) or turned my face to the sun, inhaling the smell of cut grass and noting with surprise that it smelled the same as cut grass back home. I'd listen to a lone saxophonist busking under a small bridge, peddling his blues tunes for money, and reflect that life couldn't be much sweeter.

A couple of hours later, I'd set off towards the subway to *flâneur* my way through some new borough. The sun shone incessantly, bathing the city during the middle of the day in an oven-like heat. Sometimes I sheltered in an air-conditioned diner to escape the worst, but on the whole I revelled in it. People grumbled, and blustered about escaping to the Hamptons, but this Antipodean felt right at home.

In a flash of obstinancy that lasted two whole weeks, I refused to visit the Empire State Building, or catch the Staten Island Ferry. Not for me that battle through crowds just so I could say I'd done it. No, my impressions of New York are in the details: interesting shop corners, the brick façade of a classic brownstone in the West Village, and the interior of a low-lit, smoky jazz den.

I window-shopped, and walked around the different neighbourhoods. I noted the difference between the grungy East Villagers, wheeling their toddlers about in prams and sporting impressively colourful sleeves of tattoos (men and women alike), and the thriving Hispanic, Hasidic Jew and black communities elsewhere. Or the Brooklyn hipsters with their tousled air and science lab glasses—in strong contrast with the moneyed sheen of the uptown crowds I viewed from the wide, clean pavements of Fifth Avenue, tiny dogs with bejewelled collars trotting on leashes or clutched in Chanel-clad arms.

With Fifth Avenue too rich for my blood and my wallet, I dropped several hundred dollars in the SoHo H&M on the

cheap thrills of new-season
tees, trinkets and denim,
and more in the numerous
dingy vintage clothing stores
lining the side streets of
Greenwich Village and Brooklyn. My best purchases:
a pair of battered brown cowboy boots I wore to death over
the next few years; two slips from the fifties or sixties, which
I still own—both are black, perfectly fitted, and magically
improve the appearance of any dress I've worn over them;
and a voluminous, cheetah-printed fake fur. I can't for the
life of me remember what happened to that coat, but I wore
it almost every evening for the rest of my trip—collar turned
up, a stretchy elastic belt with a huge gold buckle around my
middle, and finished off with an air of *hauteur*. I also bought

the requisite 'I heart NY' T-shirt. I know, I know, but I couldn't resist. The grungy street style inspired me—my look morphed mid-trip from polished *Friends* fan into rockabilly beatnik. A bit Holly Golightly meets Alabama, Patricia Arquette's character in *True Romance*.

My all-time favourite spot was Greenwich Village, where I whiled away the hours over one cup of coffee, people-watching and journal-writing. It captured all I'd imagined this city to be: NYU students, street peddlers, artsy types and dusty professors in stereotypical tweed leather-elbow-patched coats scanning the Strand book-store and its eighteen miles of books. I silently quashed adolescent William Hurt fantasies (he wears tweed so well, does William!), and dreamed of one day living there myself.

I still haven't done so, but there's time. I'm not dead yet.

10

SHRINKING VIOLET
(IN AN ACID-GREEN A-LINE)

I like odd people. Especially the kind who don finery each day as though life were a masquerade, creating drama and intrigue and a story to tell—from the tip of their feathered headdress to their daintily lacquered toes. It takes real courage to stand apart from the crowd and say, *I'm different, and revel in being so*. John Galliano, Vivienne Westwood, Isabella Blow, Anna Piaggi, Stephen Jones … just a few famous examples, whose hats help to create the impression of oddness (maybe because they're so rarely worn these days?). To these people I say: *Bravo!* Thanks for the thrilling spectacle. Let's have more of it in everyday life.

There's a dear elderly lady I often spy on jaunts around my local flea market. Colour blindness might account for the perfectly round circles of pink rouge on her powdery cheeks, but I don't think so. This woman is always immaculately attired in a smart fitted skirt suit and low Ferragamo heels to match her frame bag; white hair piled in a dreamy confection above her head. It's her signature look. A bit cartoonish, and very cute. She comes up as high as my cap sleeves, and I always feel like giving her a big hug and a kiss on the cheek to say *Well done, you.* I might want to be her when I grow up; she's my new muse.

But standing apart from the crowd isn't easy. To pull it off with panache you need lashings of confidence heaped upon your bowl of cereal in the morning. There's been more than one occasion I've stepped out feeling wonderfully bold, only to develop a case of the shrinking violets before the day is done. Most memorably, in a sleeveless mini-dress covered in an acid-bright cabbage print, with deliberately clashing fuchsia heels and hair swept up into a high pony-tail. I wore this to the office one day when I worked as a book publicist. I noted several sets of raised eyebrows on my way in, but it was halfway through the morning, when I went to fetch a cup of tea in the tiny kitchenette, that a tact-less colleague finally asked me plainly:

'What are you all tarted up for?'

But, funnily enough, it's far worse feeling like a wall-flower. Trust me. When I was younger and more anxious about what people thought of me, I bought beige separates because I thought I should fill my wardrobe with trusty basics (and I was going through a bit of a Carolyn Bessette-Kennedy phase). However, if you're not in the mood, beige can make you feel like you've worn a burqa to a swimsuit contest.

So, there's only one thing for it: *damn the naysayers!* Give them something to talk about. As Coco said, 'In order to be irreplaceable, one must always be different'. *Bravura* is always better than boring. Wear your animal prints and neon brights with pride, *mon amie.* Employ wigs and hats and sunglasses and bangles and all manner of other crazy acces-sories to drive the point home when you're feeling up to it.

Don those leather trousers if you love them (you're braver than me), apply your make-up with an airbrush, and face the day with a wink and a smile.

'IN ORDER TO BE
IRREPLACEABLE,
ONE MUST ALWAYS
BE DIFFERENT'

⎯᷿ 11 ᷿⎯

FASHION EVERLASTING

I've always had a thing for tattoos. I know they're *déclassé*, but there's something about the permanence of them that inspires and intrigues me, while at the same time makes me mourn for the unblemished skin the owner wore before. Whereas the rest of what we dress ourselves in is ephemeral and fleeting, tattoos are forever. Tattoos are audacious—they are only for the brave (or the reckless and silly). And, as someone who has been through so many incarnations that I sometimes have trouble recognising myself, they're a touchstone.

My father had a jaguar etched on his forearm. The once-black ink had long since leached into the neighbouring skin cells, giving it a blurry, blue-green patina. I remember tracing my childish fingers over its surface, marvelling at how the skin felt the same, despite the deep markings. When he flexed the muscle, the big cat appeared to climb further up his arm, a trick that brought to mind a strongman at a fair.

When I later saw those ad campaigns for Jean Paul Gaultier's signature perfume, I immediately adored the androgynous sailors and the reference to anchors, roses in bloom and dancing girls in neon brights—imagery of the carnival atmosphere which had so captured my imagination. At fifteen, I decided I would one day get my own tattoo, and gave myself the three years before reaching legal age to change my mind.

I found myself drawn to tattoo parlours, visiting to admire the artwork, establishing quickly what I did and didn't like, sometimes being shooed away by the owners. One even tried to talk me out of it, telling me they weren't for 'nice young girls'. The Celtic bands so popular in the early nineties were not for me, nor the blazing suns *à la* singer and spoken-word artist Henry Rollins. Nor was Asian lettering, spelling out a secret message I'd surely misunderstand or forget. I liked dolphins well enough, but thought it too hippie-dippy to wear one for life; and, as drawn as I am to skulls and Latinate Day of the Dead imagery, considered it morbid to promote this on a daily basis. Likewise, Chinese dragons and Japanese carp I admired for their beauty, but felt their symbolism too masculine for me.

Two years later and still undecided, I was flicking through a photography book in the library when an image stopped me in my tracks: *Papilio ulysses*—an iridescent blue butterfly with black-edged wings. I colour-copied the page and slipped it between the covers of my journal, saving it for later.

The week I hit eighteen, I was still convinced. I carefully examined tattoo artist portfolios until I found one I liked—Tim's at Chapel Graphics, in Melbourne's Prahran. It was a studio with plenty of sofas and a drinks fridge, less menacing than your average drunken 3 am stop-off. I made an appointment to discuss what I wanted and Tim sat with me for a full hour, sketching my photograph into a full-colour illustration, as I corrected him here and there, and we ruminated on the best size and where it would go. I chose a little patch of skin on the small of my back—low enough to hide under a jeans waistband when necessary, but high enough to reveal when I felt like it. The day my tattoo was inked, I took along my best friend, Chris, for company. He held my hand while the electric needle insistently pricked at thin skin, so close to bony vertebrae it made my teeth chatter and stomach turn.

It's turned out to be the best spot. I forget it's there, but when I do catch a flash of it in the mirror as I'm getting dressed it's a pleasant reminder, and still a surprise all these years on. It makes me smile.

Recently, when idly browsing that massive tome *The Birthday Book,* I came across my own birth date—with the exact same butterfly at the top of the page. That beautiful butterfly was the imagery for that day of the year, with the words *chrysalis, change* beneath it. I almost dropped the book on my toes. As loopy as it sounds, I feel that tattoo chose me. And I don't mind at all that when I am buried, I'll still be wearing it.

As if to emphasise the personal nature of my tattoo, apart from the first few weeks I never did wear clothes to deliberately put it on display because, well, it's just for me. And I won't get another tattoo—I only ever wanted the one.

Non, je ne regrette rien.

— 12 —

DON'T GO CHANGING

I moved to London from Hong Kong on 9 September, 2001. It wasn't a very auspicious start.

I watched the Twin Towers fall while inspecting an apartment for rent on Battersea Park Road. The current tenant answered the door with the words: 'Have you heard? It's the strangest thing ...' Her voice trailed away as I followed her inside, past a balcony festooned with pretty potted plants with cascading leaves, towards the switched-on television. Knowing virtually no-one, and left largely to my own devices, the next few weeks were spent looking for a new home on my own and feeling constantly sickened by the ghoulish news reports.

But the mood changed, as it always does eventually, and I took to my new environs with gusto. Oh, how I loved being in that hothouse of fashion! For me, London is the epicentre of street style. American style is, largely, a little preppy for my tastes. And to be chic in Paris you need to know all about cut and labels and classic staples; under-statement is key—something I had neither the money nor patience for in my experimental twenties. (Parisian 'style' is luxe and simmeringly sexy, of course, but in reality on the streets you don't see much in the way of way-out style; that said, French *Vogue* is my favourite fashion magazine, a veritable Holy Grail of taste.) Every fashion-conscious city seems to have a style code: the Milanese are always so glossily well-groomed, not a hair out of place or shoe left un-shined; and Tokyo girls, well, they look so kooky.

But London ... from the first time I visited in my teens to the day I left after three and a bit years of properly living there, London was a delirious, delicious riot of clashing tastes and colour and fun. It was offset by all that stiff-upper-lip stuff that British designers such as Paul Smith, the much-mourned Alexander (Lee) McQueen, and milliners Philip Treacy and Stephen Jones play with (and rail against) so well. Maybe it's the young people that flock there from all over Europe and the world. Or maybe it was the proximity of the famed Central St Martins fashion college; I lived around the corner and insisted on walking past it on my way to hip Hoxton, Shoreditch, Notting Hill and Chelsea where I would admire the passing street traffic ...

Whatever the reason, I was happy as the proverbial pig in mud.

But to begin with, life in London was difficult. My boyfriend and I decamped there with less than three weeks' notice, so he could follow a job opportunity in his company's head office. I'd been killing time in Hong Kong, doing writing jobs for stuffy finance and legal magazines for a number of months, after being retrenched from a dotcom when it folded overnight. My career was in a trough and I was desperate to climb out. It seemed the right time to move on.

There had been little surprise when the internet company I'd been working for shut down. My colleagues and I had been wondering when our luck would run out almost daily: we enjoyed business class flights, stayed in five-star hotels and ate bacchanalian feasts in every major Asian city at the expense of the company—all thanks to our jobs as conference journalists. But one morning we arrived at work to find the liquidators had cleared the office of all computers, phones and electrical equipment. I didn't even have a chance to download my email contact list, and thanked my lucky stars for keeping an old-fashioned Rolodex.

It had been a hoot while the money lasted, but those heady days obviously took their toll on the company coffers. I've no idea what happened to the owners, but I did learn one important sartorial lesson from one of my bosses: never stuff your hands in the pockets of your business suit or overcoat—it ruins the tailor's line and looks unprofessional to boot. If he caught us slouching, waiting for some dreary reception party to end, he'd give us a slap between the shoulder blades, forcing us to stand up straight. It was a valuable lesson in the confidence that good posture conveys: even though he was apparently haemorrhaging money, the entire time I worked for him I never saw that man stand anything less than ramrod-straight.

I wasn't sad to leave Hong Kong. I enjoyed living there for the change and adventure it represented but I didn't love the city itself, or its expat culture, revolving as it did around drinking, junk trips and dragon-boat races. The shopping was so very label-conscious, and I found myself unable to fit into most of it. Being in possession of a very average Western woman's size 10 to 12 figure, I stayed optimistic, but did not enjoy walking into boutiques, only to be told 'You too fat' or—my favourite—'Big bum!' by the tiny sales assistants, accompanied by enthusiastic hand movements (à la 'The fish was this big!'). When I repaired to the local gym, the trainer explained how my under-developed calves were too small for my curvy frame: 'You all wrong proportion,' she said, nodding sagely. I hoped something had been lost in translation.

Even though my father is English, and I was entitled to live and work in the United Kingdom for a period of four years at a time, it turns out the British Government do not like people rocking up to immigration without applying for a visa first. It took six months of soul-destroying trips to a post-war Croydon building to secure a permit. Which meant six months of temping—that most vile of ways to earn a crust—in various corporate offices around the city.

Despite the dreariness of temping, there was an upside. After months of freelancing from home in pyjamas, I enjoyed dressing up for the office each day in my fitted skirts, nifty little jackets over lace camisoles, silk tights with saucy seams snaking up the back, and d'Orsay pumps—all of which (apart from the pumps) I'd had specially made by a clever Hong Kong tailor for a song. I always topped off my outfit with my favourite bright pink pashmina tied jauntily around the neck. I blow-dried my hair every second day into glossy, loose curls. This was my riff on corporate dressing.

One temp position (my last), on reception at a financial institution, was especially memorable. Dashing young bankers sidled up to the marble-topped desk each morning, cheeky grins plastered across their faces, and invited me out to lunch, for a drink, or entreated me to join them in more, shall we say, illicit activities. The most dashing of these, a real *Mad Men* Don Draper type, was quick to offer me a position in the marketing department 'when one became available'. I gathered they needed my skills so they could crow about the firm's substantial achievements to their extensive database of private clients.

I embraced this new work environment—the return to the cushiness of company expense accounts, with those essential long lunches in thrillingly expensive local bistros —with glee. It did not take long to work out that it all came at a price ... less than a few weeks, actually, all up. My new colleagues were a bunch of misogynist pigs.

For a start, my newly created 'marketing' role involved answering phones for the department, updating contact details with the help of a handy little scanner that converted text on business cards to database-ready information, and attending business lunches with my colleagues as they courted their new clients. Easy money, it was in fact the highest income I had during the years I lived in London. Except, except ... I got the feeling they were looking for a geisha rather than an ambitious marketing assistant. I was the only woman in a department of thirteen men and my, they were a sharky bunch.

My boyfriend worked at one of the big banks but didn't move in the same sorts of high-flying, Nick Leeson-esque circles. Not only that, he was (and presumably still remains) a very decent guy who didn't much fit the stereotypical banker image. He wore lovely suits, sharp leather shoes and silk ties—but never dropped the equivalent of my annual salary buying up Gieves & Hawkes Savile Row suits, Rolex watches and various other treats on Sloane Square shopping jaunts. For most bankers, just spare change from numerous bonuses.

Slick threads and flashy jewellery mattered not a damn once these cads had had too many drinks, anyway. It was an almost daily occurrence. Eyes ogling and hands grasping, they would lurch, ties askew, red-faced beneath their five o'clock shadows, towards some attractive waitress in the local bar. They'd hilariously ask, 'Do you know how much I'm worth?'

They would regularly return from business meetings held with women in the industry (rare birds) exclaiming they could tell that one was 'crap in bed just by looking at her' or that another was an 'ugly dog'.

In the midst of all this, a curious thing happened. I'd never done it before and can't see myself repeating the behaviour pattern again, but—rapidly and completely subconsciously—I underwent a metamorphosis. Faced with the daily grind of being around these disgusting creatures I took on a new persona: drab, disappearing me. Shopping for warmer clothes in local charity stores (the only places I could afford at the time), I gravitated towards long, shapeless black skirts, thick woollen tights, blousy cardigans and skivvies. I swapped my sexy French pumps, cut to reveal the arches of the feet and tricky as hell to walk in, for no-nonsense flat Campers—telling myself they were easier to make the journey to and from work in, despite keeping them on all day. And as my first London winter kicked in—a shock to the system after the steamy heat of Hong Kong—I bypassed my cute fitted jackets for a 1960s woollen houndstooth coat with black faux-fur collar. It ballooned out around the middle and made me look like an old-age pensioner carrying a few bags of shopping about my person.

The transformation was complete when I had my longish blonde hair cropped to a severe bob. I dyed it black over the bathroom sink one night, with a packet purchased from the supermarket ... never again. At the time, I fancied the woman in the mirror bore a resemblance to Snow White with her London-pale skin and dark 'do; very fitting for a northern hemisphere winter.

In reality, it was more the wicked witch. The black brought out the dark circles under my eyes and made my skin appear sallow. When the shade of blue-black started to fade after a few washes, I was left with a hue distinctly more blue than black. The lunch and post-work drinks invitations promptly ceased, and I took to dining by myself each day. I'd read a novel over a limp-looking Caesar salad, eking out the full sixty minutes in the nearest Coffee Republic, and dreading my return.

It's only when I think back to that time that I realise quite how much my environment affected me, and how my fragile state of mind was so fully reflected by what I wore. My new dark makeover became a dowdy armour, a disguise effectively making me invisible. What did my look say? *Keep walking—don't pay me a scrap of attention.* Worse, *I've given up.* Trudging up the steps from Bank Tube Station each day, I felt myself die a little more inside as I sank further and further into this new persona, a feeling which morphed into full-blown panic as I sailed up in the lift towards my desk. *Not another day!*

I barely recognised myself, and sometimes gave a little start when I caught sight of the unfamiliar reflection in a shop window. It was a vile winter, made worse by the persistent chest infection I endured for the duration. I've been told on more than one occasion that this is a sure sign that one is carrying around too many things one is unable to give voice to ...

But as all winters do, this one ended, and so did my discontent. The trips to Croydon finally paid off and by March I had the golden ticket, a full working visa, and the freedom to apply for any job I liked—which I set about doing *tout de suite*. I applied for all sorts of things and got very few bites (depressed as the economy, and I, was) until a prominent book publisher thankfully showed interest, and after several difficult interviews that I disguised as dental appointments for the benefit of my employers, offered me a full-time job (doing real marketing this time) for exactly half my current salary.

The day I handed in my notice, I honestly felt like someone had lifted something akin to a tea chest from my shoulders. The knots of tension in my back and neck loosened almost immediately. It was all I could do not to skip into my manager's office and break the news. Given the way they operated, I wasn't surprised when he offered me a significant raise if I stayed, along with a full-time contract, benefits and a generous annual bonus. But, tempted though I was—London is a phenomenally expensive city, and my Hong Kong savings had dwindled away to almost nothing in the space of a few short months—I said no. I wondered how many others gave up their dreams when someone threw money at them. I love a golden bangle, but golden handcuffs? No, thanks.

I might have felt the first glimmers of my former self when I almost skipped into Draper Mark II's office to tell him to stick his job, but I knew the real me was back to stay when my final pay cheque landed in my account. Rather than earmarking it for rent I walked straight into a glossy boutique on my way home from work, days before I was due to start in my new position, and blew it all on a dusky pink silk kimono top. With totally impractical short sleeves, my gorgeous find was embroidered with bursting, many-petalled roses winding elegantly all over the front, and came with a gold-threaded obi belt to wrap flatteringly around the waist, ribbons trailing prettily behind. Spring had sprung.

On my last day at that sombre city office, I wore my new top with black wide-leg trousers and dangerously spiked heels. My hair was on its way to recovery; I'd made several successful trips to the hairdresser to have the unfortunate black carefully stripped. With lots of restorative masque treatments, I was back to a deep honey blonde.

So, when an Australian-Chinese investment banker slapped a thick portfolio of papers on my desk and said greasily:

'Photocopy these for me, will you, sweetheart, and I'll give you something all women want: multiple orgasms' ... I laughed in his face.

'Really?' I screeched, with a hysterical edge to my voice. '*Really?!?*' before standing up to tower over him. 'Go on then!'

He slunk back to his desk, looking fearfully over his shoulder at me a few times as if to say, *My god, she's insane!*

I stormed off, heels beating a giddy report—the sound of gunshots—on the large marble tiles of the reception area. Out those heavy gilded doors for the very last time.

───ᦗ 13 ᦥ───

L'AMOUR AND A LIBERTY PRINT

What do you wear on a first date with the man you're planning to spend the rest of your life with? And how can you even know it's him, so early on in the piece? (For the record, I think I did.) Picking out the right ensemble for the occasion is *très* important; under the circumstances, it can be everything. But then again, some things—yes, I'm talking about *l'amour,* dear reader—thankfully transcend fashion.

After five years with my previous boyfriend, Tom—three of those blissfully happy, and two miserably *un*happy (painfully aware we weren't right for each other, a fact we seemed to take forever reconciling ourselves to before a break-up as wrenching as a divorce)—I was fairly rusty when it came to the dating game. Apart from that early dinner with Simon in my teens, I felt I'd never really been on a 'proper' first date before. Australian men usually deny us this seemingly normal modern mating ritual, as most Antipodean women can attest ... Aussie blokes have a way of asking you out—for a drink, or to a film—for the first time which borders on the mates-only, and makes you question whether they really like you or just consider you a friend. Usually, it's to 'hang out' with a group of people, so it's always a surprise when things become more intimate, and you realise you're in an *actual* relationship. My god, you have yourself a boyfriend!

I had emerged from my previous relationship feeling about as attractive as a troglodyte ... a little mole person suddenly escaped out of a hole and up into the sun. It was a feeling not unlike rebirth, accompanied by the requisite bruises and wailing fear of the unknown. But the first glimmerings of hope—that *this too shall pass*—made me cautiously optimistic.

Anyway, I had no idea what to wear out with this lovely English man I'd just met. After a prolonged period standing in front of my clothes rack biting off all my nails, I ended up plumping for a Liberty-print cotton shirt and faded blue skinny jeans with cowboy boots, under a huge shaggy fur coat. I arranged my hair in a deliberately dishevelled up-do; face made up with lots of kohl and smoky eyeshadow, balanced with bare lips. It was a Wednesday, after all, and I didn't wish to appear too keen ...

I knew when James arrived at the front door, bang on the dot of our agreed time of 7 pm, that I'd gotten it quite wrong. He was in a pair of indigo jeans, but with a lovely Italian wool suit jacket of navy blue, fitted grey cashmere V-neck knit and collared shirt beneath, paired with matte leather, handmade Italian ankle boots. I was definitely expecting something more casual—a tee, jeans and trainers perhaps, under a fur-lined, khaki hooded parka that all the boys in London seemed to be wearing that year. He let slip that he'd just bought the knit, and admitted (rather sweetly, I thought) that in preparation he'd been for his first ever facial and manicure that day. He didn't seem in the slightest bit worried about needing to appear cool. He liked me, and wasn't afraid to make his feelings known. *Tick*—I admired that so much. To me, that is the epitome of cool, and it's one of the traits I love most about James, even still.

He hadn't given me any clues as to where we were going when we'd arranged our rendezvous on the phone a week before. Given my aforementioned lack of experience, I thought we'd be heading to a comedy club, or a bar, or out for a cheap and cheerful curry at the local Indian. Not so. My lack of expectation was a little woeful, in retrospect. He gave me a chaste kiss on the cheek, lingering there for a bit. Long enough for me to take in his peppery aftershave (very nice indeed), before pulling away and taking my hand in his— leading me, still clueless, down the street. Into a black cab and off through the streets of South London until we arrived in Putney, rumbling down a quiet residential street and grinding to a halt outside the front of a converted Victorian terrace.

The sign above the door was discreet—Enzo's—a fine Italian restaurant, subdued, with tea light candles in porcelain holders on the white-covered tabletops, and 1950s-era crooning piped through the speakers in each room. Not for us some showy Soho restaurant which had just received a write-up in the *Guardian*. *Tick, tick*. The waiter sensibly whisked away my Chewbacca-like coat. We sat down, with the other patrons situated a good distance away. This immediately gave us a sense of privacy, like we were the only people in the room. I couldn't stop grinning. Here I was on a real life, proper first date, like you see in films—I'd heard about these.

After an initial few awkward moments, silent while we watched the waiter carefully place our napkins upon our knees, proffer James the wine list, and the both of us menus, we smiled at each other through the flickering, flattering candlelight.

I made a snap decision: no talking about my ex, or my family, or the boring day-to-day details of my job. We talked instead of our passions: my love for travel, fashion and books and our shared admiration for many of the titles we'd both read, including Stella Gibbons's comic novel, *Cold Comfort Farm,* which James had just finished recently. (A month or so later, James would joke that one day we would be married and we would have two sons called Seth and Reuben, after the characters in the book, and that's when I *knew*. Like the old lady says in *When Harry Met Sally*: 'I knew. The way you know about a good melon.') We talked about his upcoming diving trip to Belize, and plans to row across the Atlantic, a vast distance from Tenerife to Barbados, to raise money for cancer research (a trip that would take him an amazing fifty-four days to complete with one other rowing partner, and me biting my nails back in England for his safety the whole time).

But mainly, we talked about food. I've never been one to pretend I don't have a healthy appetite. I love my food, and I really don't understand women who don't eat, or pretend not to be interested in it (people who don't love food, period). I think it shows a complete lack of gusto for one of the most enjoyable things in life, and I always wonder whether this lack of passion applies to their other pursuits. I put my opinion forward fervently: people who don't get food are not, in general, for me. James smiled. It was clear I was ticking his boxes, too. Little did I know that here was a man who took his own food very seriously—a thrower of dinner parties and lover of cooking channels, who had researched this restaurant carefully, his decision spot-on. In general, a good egg who knew a good egg when he saw one, and enthusiastic frequenter of one of my favourite places in the world: London's Borough Market, SE1.

I decided to order the steak for good measure. Bloody, with wild mushrooms in a red wine *jus* and mustard mashed potatoes to accompany it. Preceded by scallops, scalded to perfection in a caramelised sauce of verjuice, and followed by a slice of cassata, to finish. I ate every last bite, with relish.

Electricity fizzed and crackled in the air between us.

I had met my match.

∽ 14 ∾

A SOUNDTRACK TO MY LIFE

Several years ago, I was packing up my life in London to return to Sydney with my new husband, unsure at the time whether or not I was leaving for good. James, minimalist that he is, decided we would take only the necessities—clothes, important papers and our laptop, plus a small selection of CDs. The rest was to be stowed in the attic of his parents' farm in Somerset, to be sent out at a later date, just in case we decided to stay in Australia. The process was an easy one. The most traumatic decision involved which of my collection of CDs, mix tapes and old records to leave behind.

In the end, we bought about five of those big CD albums to hold exactly half of our collection, *sans* covers, indexes and liner notes. Six years later and very much settled in Sydney, there in that English attic the rest of them still live—due to a combination of laziness, a shortage of funds and a lack of space in our new home. I'm still kicking myself. I can't bear to ask my mother-in-law to go through all those boxes and post me the covers and compilations I miss the most.

My music collection is like a diary—it tracks a journey through my aural tastes and the wardrobe that went with them, even if these days only the music remains.

From the Salt-N-Pepa-inspired off-the-shoulder hot pink jumper and patterned bike shorts, to a Creedence Clearwater Revival phase which saw me dressing like Kate Hudson in an *Almost Famous*-esque Biba kit and shaggy coats. (I still have a Biba-style dress or two from back then, but not the hip hop accoutrements; funnily enough, I'm no longer fond of neon lycra.) And the embellished skirts and puffy-sleeved frocks from a journey into Spanish music— a few ballroom dancing lessons drew me in.

I'm no musician. I can't play a single instrument. Years ago, I used to take voice lessons and have, rather embarrassingly, participated in a talent contest or two. Imagine a thirteen-year-old singing 'The Very Thought of You' in a slinky black dress and bright red lipstick, hair upswept in a 1940s French roll, competing against a troupe of girls in day-glo leotards performing a choreographed routine to Kylie Minogue's version of 'The Locomotion'. Yes, that was me. Thankfully (as those who have heard me sing can attest) I gave up on the idea of a singing career, but my love of music still remains.

Music was an ever-present feature of my childhood. For as long as I can remember, our house was filled with rock'n'roll, blues, disco, country and punk. It was a diverse education; more important, I think, to my parents than anything we learnt at school. If I close my eyes, I am back with the jumpy sound of David Byrne in Talking Heads (one of my father's favourite bands), or my tone-challenged mother belting out her favourite Thelma Houston & Pressure Cooker tune, 'I've Got the Music in Me', wearing a patterned silk headscarf and bellbottom jeans, in solidarity with Thelma as she pushed the vacuum along the floor, drowning out the sound of its white noise.

Childhood summers were punctuated by whatever my parents (and by extension, my two brothers and me) were listening to at the time. Old 1950s tunes by Elvis and Johnny Cash on the way to the local pool. Sixties rockers The Beatles and The Rolling Stones (I know you're meant to be a fan of one or the other, but I don't remember there being a distinction in our house) and The Kinks playing while my parents got ready to go out and before the babysitter arrived. Or my mother's Motown records and beloved songstresses (Carole King, Stevie Nicks and Kate Bush) on high rotation well into the night as she sewed tiny sequins and beads onto the beautiful, boxy and loud jumpers she used to knit for the 1980s Australian knitwear designer Lesley Marchant.

Our parents tutored us in Jimi Hendrix with his afro, dangerously tight pants and rainbow-hued military coats, and Janis Joplin, famously all over the place in her Woodstock-era sheepskin coats and silk bandanas. We cried along with Joni Mitchell (an image of her on a record sleeve made me simultaneously want to take up smoking and cut my boring long blonde hair into eye-grazing bangs) and got down with James Brown (one man, at least, whose style I never tried to channel). We sampled Hank Williams and Patsy Cline (oh, as a rake of a girl, how I longed for the simplicity of her country frocks and homely curves), the disturbing punk of The Sex Pistols (I didn't go as far as the safety pins, although even now I'm a sucker for trashed band T-shirts and jeans, and I worship Vivienne Westwood and all she stands for), and the stoned meanderings of Pink Floyd and Cream.

Not that we were only schooled in the cool and credible. At the other end of the scale were those hit-and-miss 'Best of' annual collections—*1982 Up In Lights* or *1985 On Fire!* As well as, scarier still, soundtracks to popular films such as *Flashdance* and Olivia Newton-John's *Xanadu* and *Two of a Kind*. The high-energy dance tune 'Would I Lie to You?' by Eurythmics, and Katrina and the Waves' 'Walking on Sunshine' always remind me of my first spiral perm (the first of many, unfortunately) and my first and only pair of pink legwarmers, which I wore everywhere for a time—everywhere but to the gym.

At fifteen I fell in love with rap. I knew all the words to Run-DMC's 'It's Tricky', Public Enemy's 'Don't Believe the Hype', and NWA's 'Straight Outta Compton', and would perform them in the schoolyard along with my very 'down' dance moves, much to the chagrin of my teachers. I wore baseball caps backwards and uttered phrases like 'yo, yo' and 'word', and developed a penchant for shell suits. Sadly, I am not exaggerating. My obsession died along with a discovery of natural fibres, and when I realised the craze for stealing VW badges, like Mike D from the Beastie Boys, was getting out of control.

I knew nothing of Marc Jacobs when I dabbled in grunge but—just as his did—my inspiration came from Seattle. Nirvana, along with The Pixies, Soundgarden and Pearl Jam, were my new religion, and I was a zealot. I wore flannelette shirts over lacy slips with clumpy Doc Martens boots (sixteen eyelets, black with cherry red laces) and perched fake diamond tiaras atop my unbrushed hair. I was angry with everything and nothing, and wore my angst like a poorly phrased badge upon my sleeve.

Music is one of the tools we use to define ourselves, and never more so than in our teenage years. I wanted to set myself apart from all the other girls my age who listened to Bobby Brown and 4 Non Blondes (music I'd been enjoying myself up until recently). Having had no real conception of what was cool and listening only to what I liked or had been conditioned to like beforehand, I suddenly became The Music Nazi; a total snob about what anyone else was playing. It was a phase I didn't fully emerge from until my mid twenties when I accepted that, yes, it was possible to enjoy chart-toppers at a club with your friends, not least because they are easier to dance along to than PJ Harvey or Nick Cave.

At eighteen, I hit my Pretentious Jazz Stage, which began with my first gig at the Strawberry Hills Hotel in Sydney, and ended many years later in North London's Jazz Café. Neither venue could have been more clichéd with its beret-wearing, Gitanes-smoking groupies tapping their toes to the sound of scat drums. I moved to Melbourne, bought a black wool Saba turtleneck and skirt, 70-denier opaque tights, and studied the genius of Sonia Rykiel. I was surprised when I realised it was exactly what I first found so seductive about the jazz scene—the natty clothing and affectation of indifference—which eventually turned me cold. I still love jazz, but (for the most part) the berets are gone.

In my university years, I used to wait tables at The Continental, a jazz café and Melbourne institution on Prahran's Greville Street, which sadly closed down a few years ago. It was such a fabulous place. The staff were all either artists, students, musicians or out-of-work actors, and working there felt like being part of a big, dysfunctional family. Someone was always making a short film, sketching cartoons or musings I was convinced were genius on the inside of a matchbox, doing performance poetry in the street, or just using their ample charisma to keep the whole vibe of the place so unique. I loved hanging out there even when I wasn't working.

We were required to wear shirts, ties and braces or a waistcoat with black pants as a uniform, but with no set colour code we'd often deck ourselves out in a riot of clashing shades and prints—the very best my local Salvation Army charity store had to offer. I had a brief fling with a fellow waiter who used to turn up for dates in his banged-up Volvo dressed as a 1940s reporter, complete with fedora, silver sleeve-bands and suit jacket casually slung over his shoulder. He'd snap his fingers and say 'Hey, kid', and I'd swoon in my cashmere twinset, imagining we'd stepped straight off a movie set.

I should have been spending my spare time studying for my degree in English, but instead I went to friends' art show openings, and to see stand-up comedy and bands play at St Kilda's Esplanade Hotel, that crumbling seaside pub. We threw Mexican-themed dinner parties where we ate burritos, drank margaritas, and limbo-ed in our peasant smocks and massive straw hats to 'Tequila' until the early hours of another Monday.

One New Year's Eve at work, we had a superheroes-themed set dinner and show with Harry Connick, Jr and his band playing. I dressed up as Barbarella in a silver mini-skirt, beehive and conical silver bra with platform shoes, while my friend Rodney came as his own invention: Spanner Man, clad in green from head to toe in an Army Surplus jumpsuit, face painted green, with a massive red spanner logo emblazoned across his newly shaven head.

My favourite memories from that time are set to songs by Edith Piaf, Dean Martin, Herbie Hancock, Dave Brubeck, Perry Como and the other greats allowed on the strict selection of tapes we were instructed to play down-stairs (upstairs there would be live dinner shows featuring regulars Tex Perkins, Kate Ceberano, the Finn brothers and various other overseas luminaries when they blew into town). The bad memories—having my heart trodden on too many times to mention—are set to Natalie Merchant's brilliant and tragic *Tigerlily*, Jeff Buckley's *Grace* and Nick Drake's *Five Leaves Left,* with a bit of Billie Holiday thrown in for good measure. It was around this time I practised looking tortured in the mirror, sucking on my Silk Cuts and pinning faded silk flowers in my hair. It was Melbourne, so all my clothes—off shift—were black.

Later, I sought out dingy jazz clubs off Paris's Boulevard Saint-Germain, standing unobserved in the corners while the ground shook with the crowds' sheer exuberance, unable to wipe the grin from my face. The berets and Gitanes looked right at home there, and so did I in my Breton-inspired striped top, layered with an eighties black bustier dress from the Parisian flea markets, paired with black footless tights and flats. I browsed the local music stores clad in soft-hued alpaca scarves and plentiful kohl, my hair loosely plaited to the side, digging up recordings by Serge Gainsbourg, Manu Chao and Bebel Gilberto. From the corner of my eye I would admire the aquiline noses of the native girls, with their un-dyed hair worn long and silkily kinked to their waists, and their lovely, elegantly wasted countenances.

I met my husband-to-be at an otherwise disastrous dinner party at a friend's house in London, and he won me with a comment about how much he liked my vintage purple suede and snakeskin Terry de Havilland platform shoes— surely here was a man with good taste! He didn't look so bad himself, I had noticed, in his slim jeans, leather brogues and smart linen shirt. After a few months, he booked time in both our diaries for a day full of surprises he had carefully designed: from a morning at the British Museum, lunch in a tiny French bistro in Soho, drinks in Camden, to tickets to see Courtney Pine at The Jazz Café in the evening—the latter because he knew how much I loved it. Standing there next to him, aware he was trying so hard to enjoy those pregnant pauses punctuated by haphazard notes while everyone else in the room nodded appreciatively, I got a fit of the giggles and realised how ridiculous it all was. One of those moments when you think, *If aliens invaded our planet right now, how would they make sense of this?*

As I write this, I'm listening to Nina Simone—a Verve Records collection of her greatest hits, which I first heard at about three in the morning at a bar modelled upon Miss Havisham's house in seedy, downtown Hong Kong, complete with feather-boa festooned silk lampshades and a dusty chaise longue—and I'm struck by how essential my relationship with music still is.

Some things never change. My home is very rarely silent when I'm in it, and my car is one of my favourite places simply because it's the only space I can listen to a new CD as loud as I like, windows wound tightly while I memorise the lyrics, speakers a bit worse for wear from pumping it up a few decibels too high as I drive along.

The latest additions to my extensive music lexicon are lyrics by Canadian pop songstress Feist. I can't stop watching that '1234' clip on YouTube—I desperately want her electric blue sequinned jumpsuit, but end up settling for glittery disco separates instead whenever I've been listening to her—and chameleon-like Brit, Alison Goldfrapp. Particularly the floaty, ethereal *Seventh Tree* album, which I prefer to listen to dressed in feathers and vintage furs, hair all mussed-up and soulful. And sombre Brooklyn-based indie rock band The National's *Boxer* makes me come over all black and moody again; harking back to my Melbourne days.

The soundtrack to Quentin Tarantino's *Death Proof,* as well as Wes Anderson's *The Darjeeling Limited,* provide other, more recent favourites. 'Down In Mexico' has me bopping all over the house doing my own brand of curious exercise in biker jeans, black tee and red bandana, whereas 'Where Do You Go To, My Lovely?' inspires me to reach for a Marlboro in my white cotton and lace A-line shift, and feel all nostalgic for a childhood I never had growing up in the backstreets of Naples; wondering whether I will ever be able to afford clothes by Balmain, worn by the lovely of the song's title. Plus, I've rediscovered my early love for John Lennon's 'Instant Karma'. It's on high rotation on my iPod these days and is thus my new mantra. I sing it (loudly, tunelessly) wearing el-cheapo seventies kaftans from hippie haven Tree of Life, a wide-brimmed felt hat, Roman sandals, and a distinctly patchouli demeanour: *Yeah, we all shine on, like the moon and the stars and the sun … On and on and on and on and on …'*

My daily style still reflects what I've been listening to in the morning, a track or two being absolutely essential for that kick of sartorial inspiration when you can barely open your eyes. I look and feel quite different when I swap romantic ballet flats—thank you, Astrud Gilberto—for my banged-up R. Soles cowboy boots with steel toes, courtesy of The Cruel Sea's *The Honeymoon Is Over* or a few tunes from my favourite man in black, Johnny Cash. I still jump from rock chick, in head-to-toe black and heavy kohl, to 1960s shifts. People sometimes don't recognise me from one day to the next, as each song seems for me the point from which a whole new persona arises.

As for the CDs I pined and saved for in my teens, many of them now hidden away in that Somerset attic, they refuse to let me forget. I often see copies discarded in the discount bins outside record stores, and when I pass I'm assailed with a host of memories from the times when I couldn't stop listening to them—including who I listened to them with—and which outfit I carefully constructed to match the mood and place. They are hard to resist, and I am slowly building up my collection again to gargantuan proportions. Only these days I ask my husband what he likes too, and make allowances for his longstanding penchant for The Beach Boys when I'm not such a huge fan. I even let him listen to Classic FM once in a while, and consent to turning down the volume on my current addiction, the first Kings of Leon CD.

To borrow from Bob Dylan, the times, they are a-changin'. But I'm changing with them, too, and that's not such a bad thing. I look forward to searching through my mental archives one day, my own retrospective of all those fashion mistakes and music obsessions, because it's almost as fun as living through those moments for the very first time.

—❧ 15 ❧—

Do you love it because you love it, or because of its label?

This is a tricky one, and I find I have cause to ask myself this question all too often, if I'm completely honest with you.

I'll be standing in a gorgeous, upmarket boutique and rifling through the evenly spaced hangers on gloriously elegant racks, or staring through a store window at some beguiling display. Caught up in the clever marketing and overwhelmed by the beauty of the environment, a fever comes over me: *I must have it,* I think, palms itching to spend. Desire is stoked because I've seen other pieces from the collection in a magazine, or have connected with the ad campaign, likely featuring some stunning model I will never look like (not in a million years) whose style and effortless chic I fancy will rub off on me—*if I can just become the owner of this very piece.*

Never mind that it's never occurred to me to want for such a thing before. It might not suit me, or even *go* with any other item in my wardrobe, necessitating several shopping trips to buy all the other, costly accessories required to make it work. I don't need it, but I am needy: *I want I want I want.*

I go ahead and buy it, and have the sales assistant wrap it up all nice and tight for me, carrying my beauty home like a trophy and swallowing down the realisation it'll be cheese on toast for dinner every night for the next few weeks. I carefully open the package before me, feeling momentarily whole: sometimes the magic is all but gone. *Hey, presto, look at that!* It's just a thing. The glamour doesn't translate to my life or to me, making me realise far too late that I didn't really love it, after all.

Boo-hoo. Silly me.

Or I could be at a street market, staring at some prized designer garment displayed separately from the rest of the dross on the racks or jumble sale table, and coo to myself, *Ooh, what a find/What a bargain/I must have it immediately* ... maybe purely because I know I couldn't ordinarily afford it, not at its original price. And there's the rub: dearly do I want to be the kind of person for whom money is no object. Who doesn't need to worry about cheese on toast. It takes willpower to separate the glamour of the label (and the glamour of its perceived lifestyle) from the real and actual quality of the item laid out before me—to not be suckered in.

I'm working on my problem, I really am. And I think I've learned a few things, but only from (bittersweet) experience.

Sometimes a find is exactly that, and an incredible bargain to boot. A few weeks ago, at a flea market stall, I saw a black lambswool long-sleeve, knee-length, V-neck dress trimmed with satin. Its price? Next to nothing. A pittance. The label said Yves Saint Laurent, and the fever came over me. But, wait, I'd been here before ...

I once bought an Yves Saint Laurent jacket at a local market. Not my colour, way too boxy and badly dated, but oh, how I wanted it to work. I tried changing the buttons— no dice. I snipped out the shoulder pads but it ruined the line, and the sleeves stuck out, giving me no choice but to sew them back in or throw it away. It was too wide to begin with, the very worst of a bad era, and, after it hung around in my wardrobe gathering dust, that's what I sadly had to admit. I sold it not much later, after just one wear, but not before gambling an investment on the buttons that didn't pay off.

So, this time, I knew better. I tried on the dress and stared very critically at my reflection in the mirror, turning around a few times to catch it at its worst from every angle. A bit tight around the behind, yes, and in need of repair to the hem, but it looked good, really it did. I could cover the offending behind with a vest or a man's work shirt buttoned over it casually; to slouch about in it, giving off the vibe, *What? This old thing?* Sexy and slimming, I was sure the only reason it hadn't yet been snapped up was the soaring temperature outside, and who could bother to try on such a thing in this ridiculously steamy heat? Me. Plus it was early in the morning, just gone eight, and you know what they say about the early bird: she catches the Yves Saint Laurent. So I bought it, and I love it.

I'm hoping my dress won't bring me bad karma. Its provenance makes me ever so slightly queasy; when I quizzed the holder of the stall about why she was getting rid of such a gem, she told me her ex-husband had bought it for her in Paris on a romantic holiday and she was divesting herself of everything that reminded her of him (plus, she'd put on several kilos in the past twenty years). Oh, good. I'll try not to remember that, when I'm wearing it for an intimate meal with my husband one evening, then—neither the divorce nor the weight.

Buying into the idea of a label is all about advertising creating the want. Quick on its heels follows the need, and so it goes. I've been behind the scenes: I know how it's done. The knowledge doesn't always help us though, does it? I know the old arguments about quality versus quantity. I'm always on the search for items to transcend the current trends and last the distance, but the truth is: none of us are fortune tellers. Poor judgement and flaky willpower is all too human, and you're a stronger gal than me if you haven't fallen prey to the same spell.

But in my heart of hearts, I know that not being able to buy every single thing I yearn for is what helps me be a more individual—and less slavish—dresser. I've got a mantra now to save me from a lemming-like fate, one I carry around with me and pull out for just the right occasion. A friend once cheekily remarked, when I was debating whether or not to buy a certain designer frock on sale: 'Designers make mistakes too, you know'. Thank you, Louise. You've saved me from making a hasty decision based on the garment's pedigree (rather than its quality, or even its dubious quality) on more than a few occasions since.

—⟆ 16 ⟅—

THE FROCK OF FROCKS

When my beloved asked me to marry him, I was wearing a *très* unglamorous grey windcheater with fake-fur-lined hood, jaunty earmuffs in a khaki green, a pair of black Thinsulate gloves to stop my fingers freezing and mud-encrusted jeans and wellies.

We were at the top of a mountain in Scotland, just outside Inverness in April, supposedly enjoying a bracing romp. So, my outfit was mostly fitting for the environment, but it wasn't the setting I'd imagined he would propose in—or the stylish ensemble I thought I'd be wearing when he did. Ears too muffled to hear him the first time, the wind whistled past when I unwillingly exposed them to catch what he was saying, and my nose ran freely from the cold. The unforgiving gorse prevented him going down on one knee. But I did hear correctly when he promised I could choose the ring myself. I clapped my hands together with glee. Yes, absolutely. Yes!

Hamish and Katie, the friends we were sharing our delightful mini-break with, scrambled down the side of another peak nearby. They'd been briefed beforehand, so it didn't take long to transmit the sign language for 'We're engaged', grinning like happy idiots all the while. Dear Katie got so excited she looked just about ready to tumble down off the mountain in her haste. When they finally made it over to us, we shared a happy hug and little dance together while the gorse punctured my city-thin skinny jeans. Ouch.

Back at the ranch, a cosy weekender (an old hunter's cottage on loan from Katie's sister and brother-in-law), we popped open the first of many bottles of champagne and warmed up in front of the open fire, which was now roaring after the boys' few manly attempts to light it. James and I made several calls to share the news with loved ones before settling in for a lively game of Trivial Pursuit. We were on holiday for another few days, after which we were flying back to London. It was the heavenly break we'd been waiting months for, with our closest friends in the world, plus we'd just bought a carload full of Tesco's finest and an ample supply of decent wine to gorge ourselves upon.

I couldn't help myself.

My thoughts turned to The Dress.

One rare sunny morning, less than a week later, I caught the tube to Sloane Square. Just for a browse, really, and to see what I could see. I had it in my head I wouldn't be wearing white. Too traditional. Too boring. Too frou-frou—no puffballs or meringues for me, I decided. And no crystals or fussy bows or tiaras either, and certainly nothing too on-trend. Not the kind of dress you'd see gracing the pages of a *Hello!* wedding, if you know what I mean. Why?

Well, it was all just too ... too ... too much. We're not religious, and we really didn't crave the pomp. Much the opposite—we'd decided on holding the reception at my husband's family farm in Somerset, in the five-hundred-year-old barn, so I knew there would be muddy lanes, and lots in the way of homely charm. I didn't want too much *fuss*. If I had to define it, I was looking for a no-nonsense but (of course) still simply stunning frock. That I could kick my heels up and party in. Yes, that was it.

I wended my way down the King's Road, crossing from one side to the other, dodging black cabs whenever something caught my eye, through almost the entire shopping district before turning back again. During which time I tried on maybe twenty different frocks in shades varying from soft greys, duck egg blue and lemons, to Paula Yates red and Elsa Schiaparelli's signature shade of Shocking Pink. I might even have considered polka dots (eggshell organza featuring small, burgundy velvet spots and a 1950s-style full skirt falling to the knee, with fitted bodice and spaghetti straps). But each one made me feel I was going to a wedding, not starring in one.

Feeling a bit despondent, I couldn't ignore my blistered feet any longer. I decided to make a pit stop in a darkened cocktail bar to rest and ponder, and massage my aching calves. Bolstered by a soothing libation (something involving sloe gin, definitely), I told myself I'd have to bite the bullet and visit the scary shops of wedding dress designers. Eeek.

I should have been excited. I'd been to seven weddings in the past year alone and privy to a number of conversations about the shop assistants, who plied you with champagne before letting you try on every dress in the store if you looked smart—and rich—enough. It was a canny sales technique. But I couldn't muster up the enthusiasm for the ritual. Something perverse in me wanted, as I'm sure everyone does, everything about our wedding to be different. Unique. Out of the ordinary. And that started with the dress.

My inner selves had a stroppy little chat with each other. Inner Muriel was hopping up and down with excitement to trawl the designer shops, a couple of girlfriends in tow and my lovely, soon-to-be mother-in-law. But anti-Muriel (who is rather a bitch at times) was fighting harder, treacherously telling Muriel she was a cliché. She may even have yawned a little, for good measure, just to rub it in. I told them to please be quiet; my head hurt.

I stepped outside, a little tipsy on my toes and wincing in the sunlight, and made to float down the street back to Sloane Square when I spied it: a floor length, milk white Ossie Clark gown in the window of emporium Steinberg & Tolkien, destination of stylish London ladies in search of good vintage. It called to me from across the street, subtle Grecian draping and single buckled clasp at one shoulder revealing itself saucily as I drew nearer. Before you go all gaga, this was not The Dress. But it was the dress *before* The Dress. I faltered on the threshold, a halo of cupids strumming harps around my head, and inquired in a reedy voice as to just how much.

Six hundred pounds. Piffling for a wedding dress, really, but still high enough to draw a gasp, especially since

I'd noticed a brown stain down the front. With the mark craftily hidden by the mannequin's arm, the despoiled frock had stood so artfully arranged, draped with a chinchilla fur stole. In that moment, I came over a little huffy. This was meant to be It. Out, damned spot!

'Do you have any other dresses, perhaps something suitable for a wedding?' I enquired, entirely without hope and almost on my way out the door. 'Actually, what I need is an actual wedding dress … for me,' I added.

'Oh, yes' smiled the cute sales assistant.

I liked the look of her. She wore her straight brown hair in two long plaits, with quirky tortoiseshell glasses, and a striped lemon and cobalt raw silk tutu dress paired with Marc Jacobs pumps in beguiling saffron suede.

'You're in luck. We've got loads and they're all on sale. Up to seventy per cent off.'

Ker-ching. She led me down the stairs, to the sizeable basement where hundreds of second-hand wedding dresses, a veritable den of dreams, lay spread out before me on rows and rows of industrial metal racks. I had a moment of brain-busting overload. It was all too much, I'm afraid. I think my tutu friend sensed it. Maybe she'd seen a case of it before. I can shop for Australia, really I can, but in that instant I felt like a little lie down.

I held on to the guard rail weakly, stepping slowly down the stairs. Directly in front of me stood a mannequin, draped in the largest, puffiest profiterole of a frock you have ever seen, the exact shade of fresh Chantilly cream. This dress would have given poor Lady Di's wedding gown a run for its money, if only anyone could run in anything so insanely voluminous (and I did feel like running).

'I think you'd look great in this,' she said.

Sorry? I thought. *Are you barking?*

'Seriously, check out the fabric,' she said, clocking my disbelief. 'It's silk taffeta, which is about two hundred and fifty pounds a metre. Plus, if you take the arms away'—not satisfied with a skirt you could hide the French Revolution under, the arms were ham hocks, nay, mini hot-air balloons in themselves—'and slim down the skirt, you've got an amazing dress ... Plus you're tall, you could carry it off.'

My eyes were still on stalks. *What the hell,* I thought. *Why not?*

The tiny changing room was too small to accommodate such a frock, so I got undressed on the spot in front of a full length mirror, while she scurried off upstairs to find pins. It was near closing time and they were empty, anyway.

Now, please bear in mind I was in a weakened state. I was hungry and tired and had just inhaled a wee tipple in mere minutes, plus I was all in a flurry from the excitement of being in the marrying way, so I wasn't exactly *compos mentis*. I had absolutely no intention of buying a dress that day. After losing myself inside that ridiculous frock for several minutes while I tried to shimmy my way to the surface through acres of silk, I somehow found my way through. I stood shivering in my bare feet on the cement floor, and stared at my reflection, under horrid strip lighting there should be a law against. I tried to alter the expression on my face. Misery's not becoming on a bride.

Down came tutu, all business, and directed me to slip my arms back out from those evil sleeves. Tucking them into the sides of the bodice, she then brought the mass of fabric sticking straight out ahead of me to the sides also, and caught it in a massive, Vivienne Westwood-style bustle at the back with some pin trickery (which was lucky, because I had something like five metres trailing out behind me back there as well), smoothed a sweet little 1950s headband decorated with flat silk flowers over my crazed wisps and clutched my hair into a makeshift chignon.

'See?' she said.

I did see. The girl was a genius.

'And it's only eighty pounds, if you can believe it.'

I couldn't believe it. Sold. I might have given her a hug.

After I exited the shop triumphantly with my oh-so thrifty purchase shoved into a huge couture bag (not the couturier of my dress, who had sensibly left their name *off* their creation) there was nothing for it but to celebrate. Feeling suddenly rich, I hailed a black cab.

'Wandsworth, please,' I instructed the driver, head tipping sidewards against the window with happy exhaustion. My adrenalin levels calmed down and I very nearly fell asleep before I arrived home, celebration forgotten, and needed to rouse myself to pay and exit the cab.

The bag was so large, I had to turn sideways like a crab to make it through the front door. So much for a smart, no-nonsense sheath, hey?

A thrifty purchase does not always a bargain make, but it's often worth a go if the item has the right foundations in the first place. By that, I mean *real* quality, worthy of your fixer-upper efforts. Without that, it's not worth a penny.

Case in point.

I saw the most amazing, but utterly trashed, three-piece 1920s club lounge for sale at an auction house once. A bad-tempered bull terrier had been living on it for the past few years, which came as no surprise. Slashes in the fabric wafted a distinctly doggy odour, and you could tell it'd been years since she had been thrown so much as a loving glance. Before this unhappy life, my sofa had been carted from some *grande dame* of the Sydney social scene's Californian-style bungalow in the city's east. I guessed that her progeny had sent her off to a retirement village and cashed in on their hefty property chips. Or maybe she'd simply died. When I inquired, the auctioneer told me it had been passed in at the weekly sale for many months running. This should have given me pause, but I got all aflutter and tripped over my words to ask if I could buy it at the reserve.

'You can,' he said quickly, 'it's a hundred dollars.'

'I'lltakeit!' I said, not a thought for where it would fit.

Or whether James would love it as surely as I did, within seconds of making its acquaintance. I arranged for that three-piece to be delivered to our near-full new home that very afternoon. Not a doubt crossed my mind—I'd bagged the best bargain in town.

Now I thought I was being clever, you see, with that club lounge. My friend's husband is an upholsterer, and very adept at fixing all sorts of things, so I knew I had the man for the job all lined up. But upholstery is an expensive business, even at knockdown mate's rates, and the fabric alone totted up to well over a thousand. Plus we needed to factor in the delivery, new padding, French polish for the elegant, intricately carved wooden panels, and service fees, of course, which brought the total cost up to several thousand. Not *such* a bargain after all, but still quite a reasonable price for a properly antique sofa that now looks as good—much better, in fact—than new. It beats hands down the modern, modular thing we bought at some swanky showroom—even if the modular one is more adaptable. And it has style and character in spadefuls. I love it, and feel I'm living in *Miss Pettigrew Lives for a Day* whenever I elegantly perch on an arm, G&T in hand. I don't regret purchasing that lounge for a moment, but ... Buyer Beware, that's all I'm saying.

Anyway, back to The Dress.
I asked around among friends for advice on a skilful seamstress. One who could transform my frothy confection into something considerably more timeless, much more 'me', and drop-dead gorgeous (*mais, oui*). After

a few false starts, I obtained the number of a woman who operated from the basement of an unassuming haber- dashery store in the West End. You wouldn't know it to spy the shambolic state of her cramped workroom, which was in utter disarray and strewn with fabrics, sequins, pins and all sorts of other fripperies, but she was responsible for creating half the costumes worn by the thesps treading the boards of Her Majesty's, the Theatre Royal and various other hotspots on the London theatre map. Most recently, Valerie (that was her name) had created some of the costumes for a run of *My Fair Lady*, but she was also a veri- table whizz with alterations. *Parfait*.

I'm afraid I couldn't wait to rip off the sleeves, so they'd been unpicked and stored in an additional paper carrier bag before I even walked through the door, and my frock was in a sorry state, a bit grotty in places. But I knew I'd come to the right place when Valerie took a long look over the dress and all its features, gently brushed her fingers over its luxu- riant fabric, and declared she could see real potential.

'A good dry clean and press wouldn't go astray, either,' I heard her mumble. Hurrah!

Over the following six weeks we met for a fitting each Monday evening, and to discuss my 'options'. For a start, the skirt needed to be shortened at the back (I'd predictably done a *volte-face* on the white issue, but was still nervous about the mud, given the erratic early October weather). And the bodice was too small and needed to be separated from the skirt so that a couple of panels could be added to the sides (I've way too many ribs, clearly, and this seemed a simpler option than arranging for those bothersome bones to be removed). For this, the wily Valerie employed leftover fabric from the skirt.

Maybe the previous wearer was none too busty on her own wedding day, but below my décolletage I definitely had a Tudors-era heaving bosom going on, and fretted about a possible *heave ho*. This was not helped by the too-tight bodice, which made breathing somewhat difficult. From the edges of the sleeves Valerie ingeniously stole a pleated frill, and inserted it between the silk lining and outer shell to effectively hide an enthusiastic cleavage. The sides and front of the skirt were slimmed down, so instead of blooming out as though I had several hundred layers of petticoats beneath, all the volume collected at the back of the skirt and sat perfectly placed beneath a row of elegant, covered buttons trailing their way down the spine. Valerie snipped out most of the tulle to give it a slight *pouff*, so from the front it now boasted a far sleeker, more willowy silhouette.

And the next part is where Valerie was really worth her weight in saffron (much more pricey than gold): she came up with the idea to use the frill from the other sleeve to create a sort of halter around the neck, clasped together at the nape with two large pearl buttons. The effect was a prettier version of the Elizabethan ruff, framing the face between bare shoulders, and mirrored in the pleated frills running around the skirt at evenly spaced intervals. It was polished, but the little frills somehow gave it a *deshabille* edge. I'd never seen anything quite like it.

I'm no slouch on the girly front but I have to confess; for the great unveiling at the end of those six weeks, I felt the first stirrings of proper, bride-like behaviour. I felt positively, well, *princessy*.

In the mirror, I turned around and around, admiring its shape and attention to detail from every angle. The boning! The almost-invisible seams! The lack of any other fussy adornment (well, apart from the pleated frills ... and the halter-slash-ruff). There's no other word for it: I was in love.

I don't usually think of myself as the princess type. I do have regrettable *hauteur* at times, which I try to keep in check. Exacerbated by tiredness, it usually reveals itself in the face of officious, petty bureaucrats (I know they're only doing their job, but how can they not drive you stark raving mad when they're being so deliberately obtuse?). But I don't much go in for that eyelash-batting, *I'm-so-helpless, what can you do but adore me?* school of femininity. Of course, I know you can catch more flies with honey than with vinegar, but I'm a little irritated by girly manipulation. I'm also not fond of manufacturing drama; life sends enough of the real kind our way and it strikes me as terrifically stupid to invite more in. What I'm trying to say is: I had no intention of becoming Bridezilla. But looking back on the whole event, I've only one regret: I really wish I had been a bit *more* of a princess. Maybe that way, I'd have better photographs to show for it.

I hate to miss out on a good party. When I really should have extricated myself from the pre-wedding celebrations (a dinner the night before at an atmospheric local gastro-pub)—and said no to the second or third glass of red—to catch up on some beauty sleep and make myself all zen and bride-y, I came over all excitable. My swishy new emerald-sequinned frock and towering silver heels might have had something to do with it: I'd got myself up for a night on the town and, frankly, I was in the mood for one. And seeing those who had travelled from all over the world to be with us was such a high, and it was more than wonderful to fall into that easy conversational shorthand that only comes in the company of very old friends. Happy snaps from the evening reveal me guffawing in each and every one, in high fits of hilarity. If there had been a decent nightclub within a fifty mile radius I would have suggested we move on there after-wards. As it was, I had to be dragged from the establishment and back to my in-laws' house not far shy of midnight, all rosy-cheeked and jaw-sore from grinning. Even then, I was not prepared to say die to such a fun evening.

My in-laws had a full house, what with all the overseas guests, so my girlfriend Chrissie and I slipped into cosy flannelette pyjamas and bedded down together in the only spare double brass bed, chattering away until we finally drifted off to sleep.

About four am, I woke up again. Maybe it was the red wine, which I'm becoming more and more intolerant towards. It certainly wasn't a noise; maybe the lack of it? The Somerset countryside in the dead of night is just that—dead. And I was used to sleeping through revellers coming home at all hours in the busy London suburb I lived in. So ... what? Brain-busting excitement, more like. And the long list of to-dos to check off the list before 2 pm Saturday lurching through my head on a fairground carousel loop, despite six months' worth of careful planning.

I delicately extricated myself from the bed so as not to wake Chrissie, and tiptoed out of the room. I made it to the landing of the stairs and was about to descend when I saw the bright red alarm sensors flashing at me a few steps down. Dammit. If I tried to make myself a cup of tea in the kitchen, I'd wake the entire house up with the shrieking alarm, and have the local constabulary swooping down upon us quick-sticks into the bargain. I decided to have a bath.

I lay in the tub for three hours, topping it up every half hour or so when the water went cold. I tried meditating, before I realised I could achieve a state of mindlessness for approximately one-fifth of a second. By the time the dawn sun rose over the forest, deer standing frozen with ears pricked in frosty fields outside, I was thoroughly exhausted and just about to drift off. But then I heard the house stir, my mother-in-law bustling about with preparations, and roused myself. With one glance in the mirror, I was horrified to see the dark blue circles and puffy bags under my eyes, and resolved not to look again. So much for the blushing bride. I looked positively grey.

After changing into jeans, farm boots and a woolly polo-neck jumper (Chrissie still slumbering, blissfully unaware in our bed) I came downstairs to find M (my mother-in-law) preparing breakfast for the troops, and a thousand other things.

'How did you sleep?' she asked.

I shook my head.

We made a large arrangement of muesli, fruit, plain yoghurt and the nuts, seeds and oils for health that M is obsessed with, for all the guests to pick over in their own time. I laid the table and even had a hurried bite or two. I washed up pots and pans while M poured another spoonful of glaze over her famed honey-baked ham, and squashed cloves into its hatched flesh for our banquet reception dinner. I ducked out to the barn to vacuum the carpet, which D (my father-in-law) had been up until the wee hours unrolling and fixing in place the night before. And I pulled out the tables and chairs which had been stacked in the barn's anteroom, arranging them in two long trestles with some help from Chrissie. The boys were staying in a cosy B&B nearby and playing a round of golf the morning of the wedding, so apart from D—who had more than enough to do with the lighting, lawn and marquee arrangements to tinker with up until the last minute—we were a house-full of women. And boy, we had a lot of work to do.

The actual wedding would be held at 2 pm in a quaint little school hall situated on the grounds of a grand old chapel in the nearby town of Batcombe. Our plan was to be finished by midday, so we could share a light lunch of smoked salmon with crème fraiche on sourdough and a glass of champagne, followed by leisurely showers and lots of time to change into our frocks and get gorgeous. But at 10 am, while I was still in town having my hair arranged into a simple French roll with a few small white bud roses, the flowers for the bridal party arrived. They were half-dead, the outer petals of the roses curled dry and brown, and utterly useless. When we returned to find them unapologetically dumped on the doorstep, my *hauteur* surfaced. Dammit! Why was it so hard to find a capable florist outside of London? (See? Regrettable indeed.)

I was sick to the teeth of arranging flowers—my hands were all cracked and cut from making the displays for the barn and wedding hall from ivy, white freesias and roses, and deep pink Stargazer lilies (my favourite flowers, pale pink peonies, were out of season), with M and a couple of her kindest, most obliging friends—but there was nothing for it. M was busy with the food ... although she quietly informed me she had bought several extra bunches of creamy white roses and some greenery from the markets a few days before, 'just in case'. Clever M; that's just one of the reasons I love her.

The minutes and hours slipped away while I made a bouquet for myself, corsages for my four lovely brides-maids (Katie, Chrissie, Patti and Lisa, who had arrived from Sydney only the day before, and were all currently helping to check items off the list) and a small spray on a brooch for M to wear on her lapel. All five had conferred and—despite being located in several cities around the globe when the wedding was announced—had managed to find four frocks (and a smart pants suit for M) in matching shades of fuchsia silk; each in a style that suited them. I'd actually told them they could wear whatever they like, having always vowed I would never visit that particular brand of torture on my nearest and dearest. Chrissie wore a stunning satin frock cut on the bias, embroidered with small roses and birds picked out in thread the same shade, which fell to mid calf with an asymmetrical hem and had a *chinois* feel to it. Katie's was a long, dreamy chiffon gown grazing the floor, with draped bodice, thin straps and no other adornment bar the corsage. Lisa had chosen a raw silk sheath, a cheeky little cocktail number which perfectly suited her tiny frame. Patti wore a knee-length satin slip dress made from the duller side of the satin, highlighting her beautiful dusky features and olive skin. Paired with M's raw silk suit, I felt they were the most stylish group of bridesmaids I'd ever seen.

It was a quarter past one by the time I stopped to shovel down the salmon, and just after that when I rushed upstairs for a shower, and to wash away the grime from the morning's exertions, hair looking more dishevelled by the second. The next hour really did pass in a blur of activity, and I almost tore apart my gown in my haste to fling it on, five minutes before we left the house at a quarter past two. Make-up? *Fuggedaboutit.* I managed to apply a slick of gloss, two sweeps of hazy grey kohl in the corners of my eyes, and mascara, which I nearly forgot but ran back to the room in the nick of time to curl on with a shaking brush, while people shouted at me from downstairs to *please get a move on.*

I ran downstairs, pointy eggshell leather heel catching the ruffled hem for the first of many times that day (my carelessness would eventually cause half of it to pull away), and scooted into the passenger seat of Patti's two-seater Merc, my dear friend Scott at the wheel. He shot me a grin, and proffered me the requisite compliment, ever the gentleman.

'You look fab!'

'Shut up,' I said with my own grin, swatting him on the shoulder. 'I do not. But let's go.'

Our wedding was lovely, really it was. Once James got over the shock of realising I might not be coming at all.

We read our vows among closest friends and family—just over twenty of them in all—in a chocolate box English setting. Afterwards, we wandered down a picturesque, winding lane together, hemmed in by hedges on one side and ancient stone cottages on the other, friends trailing behind us as the photographer snapped away unobtrusively a few steps ahead. Unable to say anything, we couldn't stop giggling, bubbling over with nervous energy which gently dissipated into pure happiness.

I swept my frock off the ground as a rally of AC Cobras (James's favourite car) drove by slowly, the drivers and their wives grinning and waving at us, and shouting congratulations; we considered ourselves properly blessed. Then off to a stately home, owned by friends of my in-laws, where we were served champagne and appetisers in the gardens. The grounds were so opulent and well-tended, the owners opened them at certain times of the year to the public; it was to be kept private that day, just for us. And we had more pictures taken over the next half hour, because we couldn't bear to be away from everyone any longer, and felt silly posing. (Wedding photographers really do encourage you to stand in some awkward positions—we'd cautioned ours against it but he had a will of his own the day of the wedding, and so we decided it was easier to go along with him rather than argue and ruin the moment ... At least we managed to avoid any garter-belt revealing, though he certainly tried, and I wasn't wearing one, anyway.)

After the stressful, mad dash to the service and a few champagnes to soothe my jangling nerves, I finally settled happily into the role of bride, less-than-perfect appearance and exhaustion forgotten. The rest of the afternoon and evening passed in a dream, as we were ferried back to the farm to meet almost eighty guests in the barn's adjoining marquee, all of whom had been invited for cocktails, dancing and the wedding feast. The string quartet became a trio, after the fellow with the violin got lost on the other side of the county, but I doubt anyone noticed. It was James's turn to be nervous, and he disappeared into the house to rewrite his speech, leaving me to greet the guests in a state of high excitement.

The photos reveal a bit of emptiness around the top area of my frock (I lost 3 kilos the week of the wedding from stress and forgetting to eat and it all seemed to come from here) but, at the time, I didn't notice. In every photo I look washed out; the little make-up I had worn quickly disappeared, without a thought in my head to re-apply it, and bits of my hair escaped from the elegant style. My eyes are puffy and dark; lines are clearly visible. I look several years older than my twenty-seven years. But in each and every photograph I also look ecstatic. I am beaming from ear to ear, and James is, too.

And my dress looks magic.

Really, I guess that's all that matters.

—⟋ 17 ⟍—

SILK FROCKS AND KILLER HEELS

One thing every woman needs to know with absolute certainty is the formula for at least one outfit
which makes her look amazing. I'm not just
talking about an ensemble that flatters and highlights her
best features, either—it has to be something really special
within her wardrobe that not only looks good when she's
wearing it, but makes her *feel* spectacular as well; gorgeous,
relaxed and uniquely herself. A get-up she can slip into as
comfortably as a second skin, no matter what the occasion.
It's the outfit that conveys, to the best of fashion's abilities,
just who she is, and why.

With trends always evolving and changing, and the years
advancing on all of us like diligent marching soldiers, the
formula we arrive at in our teens and twenties, or at any
stage in life, may cease to work for us at a certain point.
We all have to review our winning equation from time to
time to avoid falling into that most dreaded of ditches:
the fashion stasis. To avoid being like those poor women
who end up the curiosities of makeover shows—hairstyles
several decades out of date and in middle age with nary a
clue—we must take a critical look at ourselves at least once

every few years and ask the question: Is this look doing me any favours any more?

Thankfully, there is help at hand, for the piffling price of a couple of coffees and a short trip to the nearest news-agency. Those clever women at the frontier of fashion do all the hard yards for us, every month, by attending the shows in London, Paris and New York. There, in the pages of each latest issue of *Vogue* (and a slew of other fashion magazines) are predictions for the season ahead. When in doubt, we only need study them with the same kind of application we usually reserve for end-of-year exams, or the wrinkles forming around our eyes with the passing of each year, and consider how we can make one or two of those trends work for us.

But this is not to say we should dump everything in our wardrobe in favour of the latest, brightest things in fashion—that way lies dissatisfaction and unhappiness. The very chicest women in the world are those who know how to update their look from season to season, without becoming slaves to the new. The kind of women who, as they grow older, retain some common thread within their style which sees them morph seamlessly through the years, before graduating into a *grande dame* with subtly refined, yet consistent, taste.

Some of us are simply too much in love with the idea of change—the giddily transformative nature of fashion—to develop a proper signature look. I know I am. But if there's one combination I can always count on, the thing I keep coming back to time and time again and whenever I'm unsure, it's this: a silk frock and killer heels.

Even now that I am a mother of a small, sticky-handed toddler, and work from home so I have fewer occasions to be seen out and about, my first port of call for a pick-me-up—even if only to swan about the house in, for a shock of fabulous when it's the last thing I really feel (and, to my mind, the need's even more dire in this instance)—is a vast rack of mostly vintage and second-hand silk frocks. For work meetings or nights out, or dinner *à deux* with my husband, meeting girlfriends for a drink and a chat or a film, this is what I wear, almost every single time. The shapes have changed over the years and the hemlines have risen and fallen and risen again, but my tried and tested formula wins out: silk frocks and killer heels are simply my ultimate fashion staple.

I find that there is something very reassuring about having a fallback position, a sort of default stance for the vast range of sartorial obstacles that face me. Dabbling in all sorts of whims with each new season—from tux jackets and harem pants to slinky leggings and simple cotton tees—I always end up regaining my equilibrium in the form of a silky frock and a pair of favourite heels. Because there will always be times when looking my best is nothing short of vital, and times when I need to trot out with utter conviction—even if it's the last thing I actually feel. Sick, tired or over it, at the end of the day it's all about confidence, and silk frocks and killer shoes simply give me all the assurance I need when that most useful of commodities is in short supply.

But I didn't arrive at my formula overnight. The thing that forced me into finding one at all was my job as a book publicist, because there were so many events—from book launches and awards dinners to tricksy meetings and lunches—that I had to steel myself for. I was always meeting new people whom I had to persuade in some way or another, either authors whom I had to convince to trust me to look after their book and shepherd it out into the world with conviction, or hardened journalists on the lookout for the next big thing, damned sure I wouldn't know it if I stepped on it. Or people I worked with who clearly thought I was too flighty by half. It was a great thrill to pull it off when I did—success!—but more often than not I started with the queasy feeling of the charlatan, talk talk talking my way into people's good graces, all the while girding myself for a knockback. Such is the mind of a salesperson—or this salesperson, at least.

A few years back, the most important events in my calendar year were the festivals and book tours I attended in the role of a book publicist. A place to see and be seen, the festivals bring together all the authors you've been dealing with for years, and those you admire and are yet to work with. You get to watch them all talk and drink and mingle for the week (or however long it goes for), occasionally attending workshops and reading sessions, while you slip around like a wild thing, huge smile plastered across your face and making sure, to the best of your ability, that everything runs smoothly. It never does.

Attending an event where two authors speaking on the same panel hate each other? Or one of them gave the other a scalding review in the national paper the day before? No problem: keep yours talking in the green room and give the publicist for the other the eye so she can whisk her author somewhere away out of view. Standing near your struggling novelist at the front of an empty signing queue, while her contemporary, the author of a bestseller, is fielding eager questions from a vast crowd of fans at the table beside them? Distract her with a pile of books to sign from the bookshop, and text your friends to come stand in the queue and say nice things to her, *pronto*. Knocking frantically on the hotel room door of your Pulitzer Prize-winning journalist, begging them to hurry up, even though they just got in the shower, because their event starts in less than ten minutes? All small fry, compared to the ones who don't want to be there in the first place and decide to make your life hell just for being the only one available to blame.

But when these events go well, it can be one big, happy love-in. Festivals certainly counteract the common image of the lonely writer in the garret, I can tell you. Unfortunately, you never know which way it's going to go.

I used to plan my wardrobe for festivals and book tours with military precision. Weeks before, I would make sure all my best frocks were clean and ready to go. If I was to be travelling to another city, they would be those wraparound silk jersey numbers that travel so well, or required little ironing once they left my suitcase at the other end. I followed meteorological reports predicting the weather, and each day laid out every item from the toes up, re-assessing in the countdown days to confirm my decision. Will this one show perspiration stains easily, or gape at the chest when I lean over? Or this ride up and reveal a flash of knickers while I'm exiting a cab? Will I be too hot or too cold if they turn

the air-con up in the theatre, or when I'm on the plane? Does it look too corporate, or beachy, or fussy? Will I look like a schizophrenic from one day to the next? How will I wear my hair?

It perhaps sounds like a ridiculous waste of time, or a little OCD, but when you have precious few minutes in the morning to get dressed, before you meet your author for breakfast because they miss their family and want some company, and you've been at a book launch the night before helping the booksellers tidy up until midnight, and you're staring down the barrel of a week of dinners and launches and parties stretching out ahead of you with no break in between for a quiet night in, planning is paramount. And looking good is the only way you're going to get through it with serious aplomb, because it's the one thing you can control, given there are so many possible permutations of an outcome in this sea of uncertainty. What's the worst that can happen? You end up the most stylish person in the room.

Disregard Henry David Thoreau's advice about distrusting any enterprise that requires new clothes; times have changed in the past couple of hundred years. But when you're feeling nervous, scared or just plain rubbish, the last thing you want to be doing is standing in front of your wardrobe, deliberating over what to wear. Or nipping out, credit card at the ready, for an emergency purchase. You're likely to choose the wrong thing in a panic and end up regretting it later, and it's a ghastly feeling to be wandering around in public, pulling at your clothes in anguish and wishing to god you'd worn something else. Particularly when your performance is under close scrutiny. So have a few outfits put aside for important occasions; clean, pressed and ready to go when you need them most. Outfits to get you in the mood—*wahey!* I'm all for colour, and prints, and a short hemline or plunging neckline (but never the two at once). Something with a little *va va voom*.

I've spent many a lazy weekend trying on all my frocks with accessories: scarves, bangles, beads and bags which sit neatly in boxes nearby, at the ready. It's not cool to admit, but I get a massive thrill when I come up with something new to make an old, tired frock look fresh. I even had James take some pictures of me in my favourite combinations once so I could refer to them in a fix. Such is my faith in the Boy Scout tradition: be prepared. Looking at a hastily snapped picture of yourself can give you a curious feeling of detachment; it allows you to be brutal about how you really look to everyone else. Somehow, it's much easier than working this out while standing in front of the mirror, photo pose on and in our favourite, model-esque stance. Face it: you never look like that in real life. And if you're a sloucher, get someone to snap you unawares and have a look at how scrappy that makes you look, too.

Heels are no less important. They should be well-fitted, so you don't end up limping your way through the day or night. But they must be killer, *mon amie*, and by killer I mean elegant and eye-catching, and preferably with a towering heel—no matter whether you're tree-grazingly tall already or barely five-foot-two. Anna Dello Russo, Fashion Director-at-Large for *Vogue* Nippon, is my muse. For the less flamboyant, I recommend you study the style of French *Vogue*'s Carine Roitfeld. And another but (and this is key): you need to be able to walk in them with a confident sashay. Not a wobbly gait. The latter destroys their purpose altogether. Yes, yes, I know how hard it is to find a pair such as these; you can spend your lifetime on a quest for the perfect shoe (or two, preferably) meeting the above requirements. But don't give up hope. I have found quite a few to see me through, usually bought at end-of-season sales and put aside for the following year because—chosen well—a good pair of shoes will date less quickly than many of the latest clothing offerings.

I refuse to wear synthetic shoes—too sticky, and blistering hell on feet, they're likely to put you in as much pain as the Little Mermaid, post-tail (and she never even got her prince, poor thing, at least not in the original). I've learned to give manmade materials a wide berth, and stick to the leather because bunionectomies aren't fun for anyone. I know women who refuse to wear heels because they're uncomfortable, but unless you have a podiatric condition, give them a go—even just on special occasions. If it means carrying those beauties about in your bag until you reach your destination, wearing less restrictive shoes in the interim, so be it. There's a name for that troublesome footwear already: 'Car to Bar' shoes. But my, how they look good in a bar! The right heels will simply make you stand up straighter, and appear more statuesque.

Commanding, rather than meek. Forget mood-enhancing drugs—these little babies are confidence in a box, ladies.

Back to the dress. Before dismissing silk as expensive and impractical, hear me out. There are so many pre-loved silk frocks to be found in recycled fashion stores, at flea markets or on eBay. An almost infinite abundance of them, languishing about after their seventies, eighties, nineties or even early noughties heydays, a bit worse for wear but otherwise good. If you like the print and the quality of the silk to touch, snap it up and have it altered, or make a few alterations yourself. A drop waist can be fixed with a belt, and a frumpy hemline with a quick *chop chop!* Frou-frou bows and frills? Give them a snip also, or decimate their number; whatever you do, wear your silk often, and don't be afraid to wear it out.

I've such a varied collection of silk frocks that an owner of the company I once worked for asked a colleague to tell him, on the quiet, if I was independently wealthy. Little did he know that most of my frocks cost me twenty dollars or less—many, a mere five dollars each—before I gave them a cheap-as-chips makeover. They'd want to, on the salary he paid me.

But I'm advocating my own winning formula only because I've found it so useful. I'm not suggesting it works for you. Maybe your own look is anything in black, or pastels, or a kaftan and sandals, making you feel as though you're always on holiday in Mustique. Maybe it's cargo pants and a T-shirt, although I doubt it. Can cargo pants ever really make someone feel on top of the world? The gold sequinned Ralph Laurens in more of a harem-style, maybe. If they do, I salute you. Whatever floats your boat, I say. Just make sure it fits.

Over my working career, I've been gifted such a nice swag of loot in the form of new and old clothes and accessories. From people I worked with who would bring in clothes they couldn't bear to throw away, but no longer saw themselves in, because they knew I would appreciate them. A friend once gave me a leather jacket, lined with gorgeous floral silk, that she'd been storing since the seventies, and a flying suit from Katharine Hamnett, along with pictures of her wearing them to parties many years before. Another gave me a forties tea dress of her mother's, too small for her, but beautifully cut and which suited me to a T. These are my entrusted treasures, my special things to keep.

And from authors—the really lovely ones who are grateful and ply you with gifts when they leave, or when you've finished working on their book and they sold more copies than Stephanie Meyer that week (rare, indeed)—I've often received something to wear, usually in the form of a handbag, or a clutch, or some perfume, or all three.

I don't mind being known for my obsession with clothes, even when it's accompanied by the assumption that I don't have much going on upstairs (which I'm sure happens, and more than I'd like to think). The really smart people don't judge you for your fashion love, because they know there's something vital about dabbling and surrounding ourselves in beauty wherever and whenever possible. Clothes and all sorts of other delectable things have the power to transcend the everyday, mundane and ugly side of living, even when all else is a bit bleak. And they help us enjoy life and enjoy simply being in their presence. They've the power to make us expansive and draw other people in.

If you don't believe me, and you don't think you can spare the time, ask yourself this: would you prefer a room with a view, or one staring out at a sunless shaft and a brick wall? I know what my preference is.

—⌒ 18 ⌒—

YOUR WARDROBE PLEASE, PRINCESS

O ur honeymoon was spent on a two-month long journey around Australia, in a hired campervan with a fridge and a double bed, kindly paid for by our wedding guests, my in-laws, my husband's savings and a meagre input from me. Two months spent on the road only for me to remark rather ungratefully at the end: *I don't do camping.* In retrospect, not really a high point for me.

I am, however, very familiar with living out of a car. Between the ages of nine and ten, my family upped sticks on a long-way-round journey in an ancient Mercedes across, through and around the Australian continent. It was a grand adventure marked by memories of crawling, on all fours, up to the ragged red edge of the Great Australian Bight, to marvel at the vast drop to crashing waves, hundreds of metres below, my father following me with stealth to surprise me with a tickle. Sugar cane fields in northern Queensland, stretching as far as the eye could see; me standing next to my brother Jack before a sea of green in a red one-piece swimsuit, the cane tops swaying over our heads as we shaded our eyes against the glare, and looked towards the camera. Behind us, a sky that was thunderous and dark blue like a bruise was rent by a jagged strike of lightning.

I had longed for James to see my wide brown country; *really* see it—not from the perspective of a city that, in the end, merely seems like most others do. Even though I had only ever lived on its forgiving fringes, and spent time in its interior on whistle-stop visits, I felt the open land was somehow more indicative of (and would clue him in to) the very core of me. It held part of my heart and I treasured it, almost as surely as I did him. Believe it or not, it was my idea to draw out our travelling as long as we possibly could, eschewing a luxurious week or two in Russia, India or Egypt to make this journey instead. Introducing him to all the places I held dear. Of course, with the weight of my childhood memories to speed us on our way, it would have been hard for any of them to live up to my rose-tinted recollections.

We arrived in Perth by plane from London, with no stopover, bleary eyed and a bit desperate for sleep. After visiting relatives and family friends for the next two weeks in Perth and Margaret River, we waved them goodbye and took to the road on our own, finally alone after the bustling activity of the last few months. That's when I made a crucial mistake: wandering into a service station to pay for our petrol, I plucked a copy of the latest issue of *Vogue* from the rack near the counter: December 2004, featuring Princess Mary on the cover looking elegant and thin.

I hadn't heard anything about the royal wedding while I was living in London—I'm not sure the British press even covered news of the Danish monarchy. But it was widely reported in Australia, of course, because the antipodeans had such a vested interest: formerly Miss Mary Donaldson of Tasmania, now future Queen of Denmark. The lucky couple met in a Sydney bar and, four years later, they were wed. The event was broadcast on national television from start to finish, a fairytale romance of the best kind.

At our next stop for the night, a quiet campsite in Albany on Western Australia's southernmost tip, a few steps away from bleached white sand and sea, I settled in to the smell of marinated chicken being barbecued by James and read the piece on Mary. Along with my glass of white wine, stowed in the van since Margaret River, I devoured that article, accompanied as it was by a glorious spread of photos, some with Frederick the Prince, some without, with growing envy. As I read on about her clothes, her wedding, her life, I became increasingly covetous of all three. Quizzing Mary about her new role and responsibilities in service of her adopted country, the article detailed the abundant beauty of the royal family's palaces in Copenhagen, and the charming home where the couple now lived, waiting for renovations to be completed on their very own palace.

I read of her sample size figure, and the racks of Prada, Jean Paul Gaultier and Scanlan & Theodore she was given to model in, admiring her luminous skin and glossy mane, unable to stop comparing them with my own beach-stressed locks and freckled nose. So dark and glamorous and wealthy—and me, the opposite, in every which way. I spent at least the next forty-eight hours feeling mightily ripped off. Why not me, I wondered? If only I had walked into The Slip Inn that night, I might have snared Fred, and the gowns, and the glamorous lifestyle. I couldn't help it;

I was puce with jealousy. The unfamiliar feeling left a sour taste in my mouth.

I am well aware of the ridiculousness of comparing myself with a possible future queen. Of romanticising her life, when the thought of learning another language and living in that cold, distant land so far away from friends and relatives would present its own difficulties. How demanding an obligation, and what a punishing schedule she must have—today I can't think of anything worse than having to be 'on' virtually all the time, and attending all those boring national events, even if I'm sure there are bonuses to make up for it. And I know full well how obscene my feelings were, in light of things. After I'd had my own whirlwind romance, snared a (non-royal) prince and been blessed with a beautiful and fun wedding, to boot. And I was on holiday for two months, no less!

But, ashamed as I am to admit it, for those next few, drawn-out days I really couldn't help myself. Standing in the dingy campsite shower block, washing a sequinned skirt by hand in a sink to the steady thrum of insects everywhere— outside in the trees, scuttling across the concrete floors beneath my feet, and being zapped as they flew into the violet lights installed in the roof above my head—I seethed at the unfairness of it all. I dreamt of a marble-covered washroom, elegantly appointed, with gold-plated taps and soft lighting, and fluffy towels made of Egyptian cotton. A logo-ed robe and plush slippers to sink my feet into. *Lucky thing*, I thought (or something a little less charitable).

I'm only human—I do think like this now and then—but I work pretty hard to avoid that green-eyed monster. How easy it is to be jealous, at a pinch. Every time I open a fashion magazine, I'm struck by the sheer beauty of the models and the clothes and the lifestyle it represents, detailed in the stories of all those rich and famous women. But I'm also aware of how it ignites my own desires, and starkly illuminates all the ways in which I am wanting. The trick is to realise the fantasy of it all, and understand it's just one small frame of an entirely larger picture. To realise there will *always* be someone more glamorous, more beautiful and more intelligent. Plus, envy is completely futile. Life's too short to spend it wishing you were someone else—no wonder it's one of the seven deadly sins.

Nowadays I remind myself on a daily basis to recognise what I already have, and be thankful for it. But I also avoid the triggers—lingering too long on a mirage-like image of what life could be. Instead I note it, and file it away mentally. There's nothing wrong with having goals, after all, provided they're within reason.

And I refuse to go camping again. Or not for a long time, at least. James is disappointed; he thought he'd bagged an entirely different kind of woman for a while there. I'm sorry, I really am, but it's just not for me.

─⟋ 19 ⟍─

ARTICULATE IT WITH ATTIRE

When I was introduced to (my now close friend) Katrina, the first thing I noticed was her severe, glossy bob and striking height. Cut with—and almost sharper than—a razor, I could tell her hair was just one of the tools she used to define herself. Her height was another, and I liked that she stood tall and proud and with such impeccable posture, because I've always thought there is something sorry about the tall woman who stoops.

Every day, Katrina wore head-to-toe black to the office we worked in, even in the middle of summer. Black, along with a flash of colour here or there in the form of an elegant silk scarf knotted about the neck, large statement necklace or bangle (usually from her favourite jewellers, Dinosaur Designs) and a bright slash of red lipstick against porcelain skin. Her workday look said strong, confident and intelligent. It also said fashion, in that perennially timeless kind of way. I appreciated the image she cultivated, which was more hand-some than beautiful (and is far more interesting than mere beauty, if you ask me). To be honest, she scared me a bit. There was something ever so slightly formidable about her from the get-go, but my, I admired her presence, which has always been nothing short of commanding. And I surmised all that from her appearance, even before we'd exchanged a word.

The old saying about not judging a book by its cover is true in principle, of course (doing so too quickly shuts us off to many new and, possibly, wonderful relationships in life), but how else are we to make sense of people upon first meeting them? Clothing might not be the full solution, but it's a form of language and evidence for the curious mind to consider. I won't claim I can work out something as complex as a human personality from their outfit, particularly since it takes such constant and unflinching self-assessment to decipher my own motivations (let alone anyone else's), but clothes still say a remarkable amount about our identities.

What we choose to clothe ourselves in hints at whether we are meticulous, easygoing, preoccupied or proud, approachable, flighty, full of discipline, or lacking in self-respect. Combined with a whole range of other non-verbal signals, our chosen garb indicates the 'full picture'. It can also, but not always, tell us whether we might have something in common with another person.

I don't believe, as some people do, that paying attention to fashion is vain or shallow—too pat, too simple—just as I don't believe draping ourselves in clothes which convey something essential about our personalities makes anything other than perfect sense. Fashion mirrors and shapes the growth of our culture; art imitating life imitating art. How can it not be fascinating, and endlessly so? It's about putting our best foot forward and presenting ourselves to the world, within a greater context.

For many of us, the most prohibitive factors to clothing ourselves in what we'd like to are money and body shape—although social mores and time constraints also play a part—but there are ways around those old chestnuts when you live within reasonable access to a city, or the internet. There's not really any excuse for looking bad and, in fact, the challenge of rising above limitations can result in some totally unexpected outcomes. Look at the street style of so many major cities: Tokyo, New York and London spring to mind. The youth culture of those places often influences the major designers, eventually becoming drawn into the mainstream, and those looks are put together on a shoe-string. And who would have thought, several centuries and even several decades ago, just before a teenaged Twiggy set the bar, that being whip-thin and bony could be seen as desirable? Or that Beth Ditto's unapologetic weight and brazen attire could again be cool, centuries after Rubens? It takes all types.

Putting time, energy and imagination into your look is the key, because there are stylish clothes to be found to suit every body shape, and every budget. Money certainly helps, but it doesn't buy personal taste, which makes style democratic in the sense that anyone can acquire it simply by asking themselves what appeals to them and why. I will admit that the more meticulous the study, the better the result. Maybe that's why lovers of fashion are often dismissed as all surface by those who consider themselves to run deeper. True, there are often more important things in the world to put your energies into. But as with anything in life, it's all about balance.

K atrina would make an excellent company head or magazine editor, because she is utterly inscrutable at times, which only adds to her polished, professional appearance and attitude. She has mastered the art of saying nothing when nothing is called for, and there's a toughness to her look which serves her well in the world of business; even more successful because it's paired with a searing wit and intellect. Unlike me, whose thoughts flash across my face without filter, and whose style could best be described as whimsical (or, from the less kind, schizophrenic).

Dipping in and out of little fantasy worlds, as I'm wont to do on a daily basis, sometimes works. Other times it doesn't. Like when I'm channelling an Upper East Side princess in twinset and pearls, to look pulled together for a meeting, but come across as plain, frumpy and aged well beyond my years—more bored, rich housewife. Or a screen siren with curves and cleavage on display in a bandage-style dress, à la Azzedine Alaïa, then have to acknowledge I might have gone a wee bit OTT (over-the-top) for midweek drinks at my local pub in an outfit more suited to an awards ceremony. Or edgy and cool in head-to-toe black, including shiny black nail polish and silver studded hardware, when I could be mistaken for a goth ... especially when worn to something like a cosy craft workshop, where a more approachable, homely look might have been more appropriate.

I am far more suited to working in my own environ-

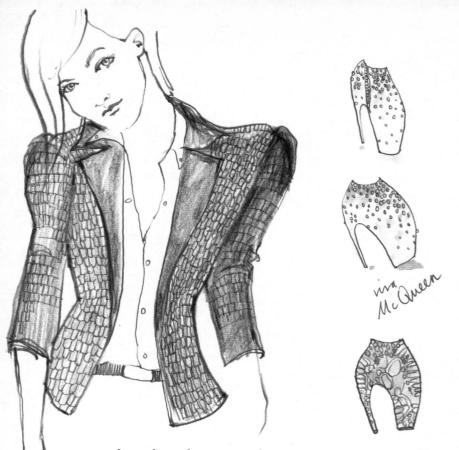

viva McQueen

ment—where the only opinion that matters is my own, and I can wear a riot of clashing colours and prints every day if it pleases me (which it does). Even if it means I am in danger of becoming ever more eccentrically dressed as time goes by.

As each season passes in a merry-go-round of changing fashion whims, with me hopping on and off board whenever I see fit, Katrina's style rarely dates or changes; just like those impeccably dressed women who rock up to Paris, London or New York's fashion week every year in their signature black, while the models look more and more outrageous, and then completely wrong within a few seasons' time. I won't lie: I prefer the models, but that's what makes me such a sucker for fashion. I'm the perennial consumer—always agog at the lavish performance and colourful drama; the spectacle of the new. Someone like me does not make a good leader in your traditional work environment. I'll admit it, I'm too inconsistent. You can tell just to look at me, same as you can tell Katrina would be a seriously safe bet.

As I came to know Katrina and we became very good friends, something I read once in a novel came to mind. A male character tells his ex-girlfriend one thing he's learned about women, and the crux of it is this: those who appear all strong and independent on the outside have a soft flesh beneath the hard exterior, a vulnerability you can count on. Just as the frothier types have a vein of steely determination running through them, sure as death and taxes. There's a lot to be said for first impressions, and I know I'm contradicting myself somewhat, but I think there's some truth to the notion of the exterior-interior self.

For (with permission) I'm giving away one of her secrets here, but Katrina tells me that the more nervous she feels, the stronger she'll aim to dress in the morning. If she has an important meeting or unpleasant day ahead, she uses her clothes as though they are armour—to summon up courage when the real thing has abandoned her. It's almost as if she's constructing a carapace to shield her from the worst of it, an outfit to soldier into battle with. And indeed, another friend spied her stalking through town once on her way to a meeting, and described her in hushed tones as amazingly elegant, but fearsome in full regalia. How about that? Clothes to shield our weakness or misgivings, and clothes as weaponry.

I understand the concept, even if my own attraction to clothing feels more subconscious and organic, something I can deconstruct fully only in retrospect. I'm more about referencing my influences—coming up with little stories in my head like I mentioned earlier. Of course, for a night out, I'll always put together an outfit to herald the fun I intend to have (particularly if I'm feeling washed out and more enthusiastic about a quiet evening in, in front of the television, or propped up against many pillows in bed with a good novel), more than for the way I'm feeling in that very moment. Who doesn't? Even in my less enthusiastic moments, I know the evening will be spoiled in the wrong frock, so I think hard before choosing an item which forces me to live up to its personality. It's a good trick, because fun often follows suit, even if, on occasion, my frock ends up wearing me and not the other way around.

We use clothes to reflect the emotions we're feeling—floaty, whimsical, vivid, sombre or simply up for a party—but there are times when clothes can be employed for subterfuge, and to project the image we want to display. If clothes maketh the man, then we can decide upon the (wo)man we want to be. Gatsby knew it, for why else did he take such pride in those meticulously made silk shirts? Dressing for the job you want, rather than the one you already have. You notice it a lot in the more cutthroat of work environments—among people who work for investment banks, say, and in law firms. At different points within our lives, clothes can reveal our greatest aspirations.

And never more so, of course, than socially.

_ᱬ 20 ᱪ_

STYLE IS CONTEXT

The places we call home, their customs and mores, become intrinsically woven into our DNA. Maybe at first they represent who we want to be, before forming part of who we are. But at some point, the two are inextricable, even as we move on elsewhere. To a certain extent, they define us, and we clothe ourselves in their influence—both literally and metaphorically. Everywhere I've lived, I was still _me_, walking around with the same sensibilities—but I altered what I wore to accommodate the light and the season and the _je ne sais quoi_ of the place I was in. A new, subtly enhanced version of myself, irreversibly changed.

My mind's eye always associates Sydney with refracted light, broken beams twinkling on the harbour or bouncing off skyscraper windows. City lights on the midnight water, or fireworks reflected in shop windows along Chinatown's Dixon Street. Being outside, traversing the winding streets, coves and hidden places of the Balmain peninsula where I spent most of my childhood, and then as a teenager, on foot. For a city girl, it wasn't your ordinary average urban existence, but that's Sydney in a nutshell for you. There are wild places to be found all over.

As a *flâneur*, my thoughts were usually occupied by the outdoors environment, rather than the interiors. Taking circuitous routes past tightly packed houses on my way home from school, I chose the long way round to decide upon a favourite dwelling and imagine the person I would be, if only I lived there. My dreams usually took the shape of a modest sandstone cottage with wraparound porch. Cool and dark within during the long, hot summers; cosy in winter and overflowing with possessions collected during a lifetime of journeys to foreign places. I coveted the wardrobe of a well-travelled adventurer: sandals from Marrakech embroidered with gold thread, Indian kaftans in shades of sage, violet and saffron, and Thai silver jewellery, layered over Parisian underwear and satin slips, and sexily enhanced by liquorice eyes swept with Egyptian kohl. Maybe my dream took shape after spying something as banal as the owner arriving home from the supermarket, or an old black and white photograph of a wildly clad bunch of hippies from the sixties.

Balmain still has so many of these buildings, worker's cottages the legacy of its docklands past. And White Bay Park, a forgotten little patch of land behind the still-working docks, which I knew like the back of my hand, and still recall clearly. In the time before I learned to drive, my knowledge of Sydney was limited to this area and other places on the Inner West public transport bus routes: Rozelle, Glebe, Leichhardt, Annandale, Bondi, and the city itself. I travelled light, collecting sights and folding them up like origami cranes to store in my pockets for later use.

Melbourne was my first adoptive city; the first place I fell in love with, when given the choice. I loved it for its cooler climate, grungy cool, proliferation of hole-in-the-wall bars and cafes and its obsession with fashion—which appeared so much closer to the Europe of my imagination than my sunny home town had. I moved there when I was eighteen, and the feeling of discovery never left me. This has formed part of Melbourne's perennial allure for me.

When I lived south of the border I came to wear black almost every day. I overdosed on it. It wasn't just because black was the overwhelmingly prevalent anti-colour to attire yourself in, or the instant way to sheepishly fit in with everyone else, although certainly there must have been an element of that. Something about that city inspires unflinching contemplation of cut and intricate detailing, and one sombre shade to contemplate it in is more than enough. By all means, study the minor subject of charcoal or indigo, but for a short time only because black is *always* the new black.

There are stores in Melbourne where every item hanging on the rails is black, maybe broken up with a white shirt, or chocolate coat, or forest green boots. The mind shuts down and reassembles—in a store like that, nothing 'catches the eye'. And yet ... it's like looking at a Magic Eye image. You don't see it, you don't see it, you don't see it and then ... you do. Much like Melbourne itself. In my opinion the city is, at first glance, unlovely. But it inspires such creativity and mellow thought, revealing itself to you as a shy lover would if only given half a chance.

It's an indoor city, where my special places are all interiors: the aforementioned tiny bars, shops, cafes, and
the additional share houses where I explored the recesses
of myself and came to understand more about the inner
workings of other people than I'd cared to previously. That
is my Melbourne—largely devoid of geographical compass
points save for Flinders Street Station, Brunswick Street,
and St Kilda Pier. I'm still confused by which suburbs lie
to its four corners, even though I visit a few times each year.
This does nothing to stop me finding new, hidden gems to
love every time I do.

Years after going too far and issuing a *fatwah* on black
in my wardrobe, I've started to build up my collection
again—but only after a break of more than a decade, and
because I've accepted how very slick, and very useful, it is.
Still, the city has left an indelible imprint upon me. Black
comes in a wide variety of shades, that I know. And is the
staple, nay, the backbone of any wardrobe. Melbourne
taught me that first, and I haven't forgotten her lesson.

A doptive city number two was Hong Kong, where I lived
for less than two years. Circa 2000 and post-
handover back to the Chinese Government, I remember
sequins, silk-satin, diamantes and Swarovski crystals;
stamped Tiffany silver draped about the neck and a
weighty rock on every left finger. It was my first true taste
of bling because, despite the breathtaking poverty to be
found in certain places, Hong Kong dripped in its gaudy
wealth. Full of pungent smells, unforgettable daily sights

and a brash excess which assaulted the senses, as a city it sizzled; a glittering jewel on the fragrant harbour. After the sombre minimalism of Melbourne, I welcomed its unashamed brashness, once I felt able to take it in. But my Hong Kong life was that of an expatriate, and I don't claim to have properly understood its real identity for even a second.

I read *The World of Suzie Wong* and developed a love of cheongsams, even though so few women donned the traditional fitted silk dresses in the former British colony. Unable to find anything I liked in my size stocked in the stores, I had them made to order, with fabric designs as varied as those in Wong Kar-wai's wonderfully atmospheric film, *In the Mood for Love.* I amassed a collection in glittering gem shades and unusual retro prints found on the mainland (only seven minutes on the Star Ferry, it still felt a world away), and wore them to all sorts of occasions from high tea at the China Club to pre-prandial drinks on a hotel rooftop, overlooked by the shadow of Victoria Peak.

While the affluent island-dwellers looked to Europe and America for sartorial guidance, draping themselves in Louis Vuitton, Gucci and Ralph Lauren—markedly different from the mainlanders, who were still suffering from the effects of Mao's

Cultural Revolution (something that sounds far more benign that it actually was)—I sought something quintessentially Chinese from Shanghai Tang and the other local designers who celebrated China's style, before communism dictated everyone wear the same tiring shade of khaki green. My way of assimilation marked me as an outsider, but I couldn't have looked more out of place anyway, with my blonde hair, curvy frame and unusual height. As an expat I would never fit in, so I revelled in my own version of a uniform.

My Hong Kong was unavoidably gauche, but so beguiling all the same. I learnt to add layer upon layer of embellishment, to drape myself in costume sparklers (never the real thing) with pride and—in short—to dress up. I mean, seriously *go to town*. I wore wigs and feather boas and towering heels. I'd arrive home to my high rise Mid-Levels apartment at dawn, shoes clutched in one hand as I stumbled into bed for the few hours before I was due back at work, pulling a black silk eye patch over my weary peepers. At work from 8 am to 8 pm most days, I really lived in that city by night.

And then London. Ah, scrubbed English Rose faces set against cashmere. Wearing hats well. Boots and gloves and belts and bags. Pretty, unkempt eccentricity; tweeds in age and in youth. My London was cleft in two.

At work, it was all about the accessories, and pared-back simplicity. A scarlet coat against grey or dark emerald boots. A peacock blue beret, which looked so fetching against dirty buildings pasted with graffiti-ed, peeling bill posters and those low London skies. Simple suits which took me through the weekdays, and served me well in the early evenings when I met friends for a cocktail or two in my local neighbourhood bar. On the tube we were one, us city-bound ladies turning day-to-night dressing into an art form, maybe popping in at Topshop for a brooch or something fun to brighten up the post-work evening on the way home. The fashion chain's train station outlets always reached a bustling crescendo at about six. I drew the line at mixing the commute with the taking of my daily exercise— a slick skirt suit and burgundy opaque tights paired with trainers was definitely not for me.

At play, I found eclectic layering worked a charm. The city with street style in spades, I've never turned my head so often to stare after strangers. Who needs a magazine for inspiration when you're tripping through the pages of one every day? Those young women around Central St Martins, Portobello Road and the East End's Brick Lane I adored the most, and I was simply drawn to the King's Road as the moth is to the flame. But, oh, the midweek polish versus the carefully dishevelled, streetwise look on the weekend … Just one of its many contradictions: uptight and undone, class-conscious and unashamedly dissolute, London fashion runs the full gamut.

On weekend mini-breaks out of town, I came to recognise and adore the elegance of chic country dressing, à la the Queen at Balmoral. Hunter wellies and Barbour coats, the exact shade of heather green. Houndstooth flat caps and tan Nubuck driving gloves. Chunky Aran-style knits worn over layers and layers of softest wool, and tartan kilts. I longed to step out from the pages of the Brora Scottish cashmere catalogue, minus the long-haired Highlands cow for company. My friend Katie had the look down to a T, and she cemented my appreciation of quality and the glory of natural fibres. When we shopped together, I couldn't help myself; I was always drawn to the bright sparkly things reeling me in with their siren song. The latest fad on the rack. Beside me, Katie would rub every item between fingertips, eyes closed, testing for quality, sometimes emitting a satisfied *hmmm*. Rarely did she buy, but when she did, she chose well.

Home again, after London. Why did I return? Maybe those wretched Qantas ads reminding me to still call Australia home. It's a cold-hearted expat—or a liar—who insists they don't bring a lump to the throat.

After staying away for the better part of a decade and for the longest in London, the city that captured my heart, I finally came to appreciate Sydney for its wonderful lifestyle and undeniable beauty. If not a truly international city, given its sheer distance from *LondonParisNewYork,* it still values fashion and commerce and fun to be had, without the ominous crush of the Underground. Plus, I think it's become a more fashionable city over time. So many Sydney designers are now successful overseas, effectively putting us on the fashion map. Ksubi, Kit Willow, Camilla and Marc and the duo behind sass & bide, to name just a few. Their Fashion Week collections have been going down a storm in the northern hemisphere, and with items now stocked by Net-A-Porter and worn by starlets and clothes horses alike across the globe, one doesn't really need any further testament of Sydney's style significance.

I whispered to my husband-to-be of living in a city where one always felt on holiday. The south of Spain minus the siestas, and the tricky learning of Spanish. After several London winters I longed for the climate, even as I longed to stay put. I was never bored with London but, oh, how I missed the light and the warmth of sun on my skin! The colour of eucalypt trees caught in a burning orange glare during the golden hour. Could I love it enough to swap it for a London cocktail hour? Turns out, I did. I ached at the thought of leaving my beloved London behind but it was time for a change; I could sense it in my waters.

Since returning, I've adopted a freewheeling bohemian, experienced traveller style I can't shake. Not dissimilar to the woman in the sandstone cottage of my adolescent dreams. What some might call hippie luxe, it's less about an education in black, or razzle dazzle, or impeccable quality and chic layering; it's all these things thrown together, which so works for me here in Sydney. Maybe it's not the city I'm in, but the mix, now irrevocably woven into my acquired fashion profile.

Today, this city suits me perfectly. It is my best foil, and my favourite outfit. I fancy staying a while.

— 21 —

CLOTHES IN AN EMERGENCY,
AND CLOTHES FOR COMFORT

A few years ago, I went through one of the saddest, most difficult times in my recent years. My younger brother Will, who was twenty-one at the time, was involved in an accident while riding his motorbike home from work.

It was about 6.30 pm when my other brother, Jack, called in absolute shock. James and I were eating an early dinner at the time, it being a miserable, cold mid-winter night. The rain was slashing sideways, and the wind howled about the house, hurling the branches of nearby trees violently against our windows. I don't remember Jack's exact words, but he gave a low, guttural moan that I'll never be able to forget. A four-wheel-drive had turned into the road Will was travelling along at speed and, without seeing him, ploughed directly into Will's side. The accident was bad. One leg was smashed and Will had been taken to hospital by ambulance, and could we come help Jack clear up the debris from the road, *please?*

I was wearing jeans and a tee, which I'd changed into upon arriving home from the office, and grabbed the first thing I could find to fling over them: my red trench coat, which I'd worn to work that day and left hanging over the back of a chair nearby.

We arrived on the scene—a busy road, with cars whizzing by in the wet dark—to find clothes lying along the gravel, covered in thick clots of blood. They'd been cut from his body by the paramedics, before they loaded him on a stretcher and drove him away. His helmet lay cracked and lolling on its side in the gutter, and his bike was scattered in bits across the road and on the pavement. Jack was on his mobile phone talking to someone as we approached, hands waving in the air and looking like he didn't know what to do with himself.

We helped clear up the mess on the road as best we could before making our way to Emergency. When we got there, one of the surgeons on duty told us they would have to amputate Will's leg. I think I nodded, then promptly sat down on a hard plastic chair nearby, sure I would faint or vomit or do both. The fluorescent-lit scene swam before me; I felt like I was underwater. I vividly remember Will's screams and watching him thrash about on the bed, surrounded by nurses and doctors, as he yelled at the top of his lungs not to take his leg. It was one of the most awful things I've ever seen.

A team of doctors worked all through the night to save his leg, purely because of an encouraging sign in the form of his healthy pink toes. Even though his leg had been pulverised from knee to ankle, and the bones in his thigh were internally crushed, blood was still reaching his foot and they might, just might, be able to save it from amputation. They grafted a vein from his good leg to the bad one, because he'd completely destroyed a major artery, and put him in an induced coma. Sometime after 1 am, we were told to go home.

Our family, internecine and disjointed at the best of times, pulled together to make sure we could be there in shifts to keep Will company over the next few weeks. My manager was very understanding, as I took off quite a lot of time to be with him. Mercifully, the doctors saved his leg. But they left a gaping hole covered with gauze while they decided how best to deal with it, eventually covering it with skin and muscle grafts from all over his body, in a gruelling, eight-hour operation two weeks later. Will then contracted the dangerous golden staph infection, which slowed the healing process and meant some of the grafts didn't take. I've lost track of how many operations he had in the following months, all the while bedridden, and then in the following few years as he battled through physiotherapy. I don't want to ask him; I know he's sick of speaking about it.

But I do remember that I wore that red trench coat again to see him in hospital. The trench (which I've since given to my neighbour, Emily, as it far better suits her lovely pale skin and dark locks) was blood red. The colour of a fresh wound. It startled me to realise this when I was sitting by his bed in the intensive care unit a few mornings after the accident, watching him sleep. I don't know what possessed me to wear it again, this coat the colour of gore. I felt queasy when I realised, and took it off immediately, rolling it into a shameful ball before pushing it to the bottom of my bag, fretting about what the doctors and nurses would think, and (more importantly) Will if he woke up. I wanted to protect him from memories of the last time he'd seen such an abundance of red.

There is so much about our response in unnatural circumstances that bears scrutiny. Being who I am, I think about clothing. How do we get dressed when the world seems to stop, and our focus narrows to the precise thing causing us distress (and nothing else) for a time? Clothes become no better than rags, simply there to cover our nakedness, in the first instance. How can we possibly attempt to make ourselves look good? And is it a form of sacrilege?

In times of stress, we tend to seek comfort in a cashmere cardigan or a pair of soft, well-worn tracksuit pants. And recovery, or at least the lessening of pain over time, is signalled by a renewed interest in our appearance.

At least, that's my experience.

Yesterday, I was driving home from lunch and a shopping expedition because it is now early January and I am weak-willed when it comes to the sales. Driving along in the outside lane and directly next to a bus down a busy main road, I was travelling towards the centre of town when the bus next to me indicated and then pulled out into my lane. I braked suddenly, because the bus was about to cut me off, and watched in horror through my rear vision mirror as a man on a bicycle coasted down the hill towards me at speed, rammed into the back of my car and flew up over its top, before falling down to the right-hand side and into another lane of traffic. Fortunately, the cars in the other lane had slowed, but all around us brakes screeched as cars pulled to a halt. Somehow he had managed to avoid being hit.

With shaking hands I opened the door, scrambled out and, with the help of passers-by, shifted him to the footpath before moving my car around the corner and out of the way of banked-up traffic. Two girls in school uniform were sitting by his side when I returned, taking it in turns to ask him if he was alright. He told us he was, in a groggy voice. A long graze along his right arm, already swollen and beginning to bleed, was the only injury I could see, but he told us he had hurt his knees when he had fallen, and hit his head. Indeed, his helmet was lying on the ground nearby and I wondered how much use it had been.

The cyclist insisted he was okay, but then tried to sit up. His entire body shook with convulsions and his eyes rolled back in his head before he slumped back down to the footpath, skin turning grey before us. All I could think was that he had concussion, broken legs ... or worse. I called an ambulance using my mobile, punching at zero three times, only just remembering where I was and that it wasn't nine-one-one.

I somehow managed to explain where we were and the operator took my mobile number, advising that she would send an ambulance immediately. As I crouched down next to him, telling him I was sorry for not being more careful, I was so full of regret and crazy anger with myself; I felt so responsible. As I replayed the point of impact over and over in my head, my stomach lurched, sick at the thought of everything that could be wrong with him.

However, to be honest, in that moment I couldn't stop thinking about what I was wearing. More to the point, how utterly stupid I felt in my lacy black slip dress and grey cardigan, with black footless tights and gold and black glad-iator-style leather sandals. How inappropriately dressed for a situation of such gravity! I don't know what would have been more fitting—no-nonsense jeans and a T-shirt, maybe—but I distinctly remember that I was embarrassed by my appearance, even though it had been perfect for my little jaunt around the shops. And looking back, I can't help but think what a strange realisation that had been, under the circumstances.

Thankfully, an ambulance officer arrived on a motor-bike a moment later, followed by two in an ambulance. They checked him out all over before announcing that—apart from a mild case of shock and a few bruises—he was fine. The one on the motorbike, a big burly type, then asked me if I was okay. Rather embarrassingly, I burst into tears. What an idiot. After a while they all waved me away, insisting it was okay for me to go, and I remember the poor cyclist consoling *me,* and telling me not to cry.

When I got home, I changed out of my outfit and into a pair of pyjamas, before lying on the sofa. I curled myself up into a ball for a while before I could summon up the courage to call James and tell him. I felt soothed by my clothes. The presence of soft fabric, after the unforgiving hardness of the road and the footpath and the scene.

I remember the phase I was going through—working a strange look of pale silk pyjama bottoms and hand-dyed spencers, along with wooden clogs—when I was a teenager and my uncle died suddenly at the age of fifty-four. An alcoholic, he went into a diabetic coma while he was sleeping and never woke up. The neighbours discovered him a whole two weeks later, from the smell. It was unspeakably awful.

I was nineteen, and wore one of my current outfits on the plane to attend the funeral, covered with some retro jacket, my shoulder-length hair twisted up into little knots on the top of my head like Bjork in the 'Big Time Sensuality' film clip—a thoroughly nineties, rave-inspired 'do. But what *is* fitting for a funeral when you're nineteen? If I could go back I'd be changing into a nondescript little black suit, hair pulled into a bland ponytail, eyes downcast, no clogs on my silly feet.

— 22 —

THE PERFECT ANTIDOTE

Here's my cure-all for when you're feeling low. Turn off your mobile phone, unplug the computer from the wall, and run yourself a bath. The world can wait.

Grab a treasured novel from the shelf. My all-time favourite, comforting books for when I'm sad are *Brother of the More Famous Jack* by Barbara Trapido, and Jeanette Winterson's *The Passion*. Choose something that makes you smile, and feeds your soul.

Make a cup of tea, or pour yourself a favourite beverage. Champagne for me, please.

Get naked and hop on in the tub. Sink down as far as you can without getting your face wet; glass in one hand, book in the other, towel at the ready for when you spill one or drop the other. Now read. And drink.

When the water starts to cool, and you can feel the knots of tension in your body have melted away, get out and dry yourself off.

This is the most important part: what's your favourite outfit? Not for going out, not that one. Your comfiest, kindest look for lounging. A pair of soft cotton trousers, the ones that don't pinch anywhere, over silk knickers? Where's that cashmere cardigan you blew a week's salary on? The one that feels like heaven to the touch and says 'safe' more than a tightly-wrapped babe.

Pad around the house serenely. Maybe curl up on the sofa or bed for a spot of quiet contemplation, or continue reading your book. There you go, isn't that better? Even nicer than a good night's sleep.

—⁊ 23 ⁊—

MY GRANDMOTHER'S SUIT

There is a black and white photograph of my grand-parents, Claudio and Isabella, which I am forever drawn to. It lives in a small frame hanging in the alcove of our hallway, along with several other black and white pictures and a selection of collages, postcards and prints I've collected over the years.

Claudio and Isabella are at a wedding, seated at a round table, with people blurred in the background. Half-filled wine glasses sit before them, and their faces are serious, thoughtful, and turned in profile towards someone off to the left. I'm sure it was taken during a speech.

With her Croatian background, my grandmother was dark and a little heavy set. In this photo she wears her womanly weight well; all curves and softness, dark hair in curls around her face. She died when I was eighteen, and in my living memory she was always wearing flower-printed house dresses which billowed out to hide her bulk beneath, and her hair was dyed a chestnut brown, which was not so hard on her lined face.

As a younger woman, it is clear she had a taste for finery—pillbox hats with gloves and elegant heeled shoes;

a matching clutch to complete the look. There's something distinctly natty about her attire and the way she put things together—more than what was simply commonplace for the time. Her posture was very good. I have seen other pictures of her, before and after the Second World War, in tailored pencil skirts, suits and dresses which flattered; did proud her figure in those times when curves were a feminine ideal. She was a determined woman—you can tell by the set of her jaw—who survived a Nazi concentration camp. She also had strong, prominent cheekbones and a well-defined chin. When I look closely I can see so many other faces in hers: my mother's, both my brothers', and my own. Occasionally I catch one of her expressions in my daughter's face, just a glimpse, and she is alive once again.

In my black and white photo she is wearing a fur stole and a cocktail hat, which matches her frock. Both the hat and the frock are in a pale fabric, decorated with small floral sprigs. The fur must be brown—fox, I'd guess. I bet it had an orangey tint. My grandfather, sitting next to her, is in a dark suit. Not black. Navy, I think, with a white shirt and black tie beneath his slim-fitted jacket. He looks handsome, and is shorter than her. Dark and Italian, always brooding with that hooded brow and large, dark eyes with circles like bruises underneath, hair slicked back like a member of Sinatra's Rat Pack. And there they are once again, those same faces of today, spied in his stare of yesterday. My grandparents' strong genes have all but obliterated my English father's line, except for our colouring, which is mostly fair.

My grandparents were quite old, in their late thirties, for the era in which they married; older than I am now, and I've already been married more than five years. My grandmother was wed to another man before the war. But he was lost, he died—I don't know how—sometime during those years. And they had a son, my uncle, also lost for three long years but then found again. My grandmother collected him after the war ended, picking his face out from endless film reels of children, shown in a theatre in London's Leicester Square. This was long before she had my aunt, and my mother, and before her second marriage ended, too. Everyone always wondered how it was she could be so sure it was her son on that theatre screen, but to my knowledge no-one discussed it with her directly; these things were left unsaid.

Nothing remains of my grandmother's early wardrobe. All I have is pictures, and a desire to re-create one of her fine suits.

In one photo she is smiling at the camera, careful not to show her teeth, in an unusual show of informality. I can see that she is joking with the cameraman—maybe flirting— outside a dark wood-panelled store, somewhere in Europe, on the street. She must be about twenty, I think. Her jacket is buttoned with covered fastenings to a high neck at the side, almost military in style—it's the frogging that gives it such a feel. It is light, a shade of grey in those black and white photographs which works well with her suit. What colour it really was, I can't tell. With rounded shoulder pads tapering down to thin cuffs, it is paired with a long shapely skirt covering her knees; probably made of wool, or maybe a silk mix. I imagine that skirt has a little fishtail, some sort of kick at the back, and maybe a few large buttons—decoration—to match the buttons at the top of the suit.

It is important for me to notice and pick out these small details, finding beauty in them and beauty in the way she lived. Rather than dwelling on her raised voice in all the arguments I witnessed over the years, and her slow decay, seeing that smile of hers gives me such relief. After a decade spent assiduously forgetting, I have decided to have that suit made as a celebration of her early pleasure in fashion, which I now share. And because I've been searching for a flattering pencil skirt for years without success. I doubt I will wear both pieces of the suit together often, instead separately—the jacket over a soft cotton tee and slim jeans with heels, say, or the skirt with my oyster-coloured cashmere cardigan and chignon when the mood takes me to appear a little more refined.

I am keeping an eye out for the perfect fabric and will have it constructed in a French grey—maybe lined with silk, a pale pink. And when I wear it I will remember her in her prime. At her very best, and no less.

Onwards and upwards, as they say. If we don't learn from the past then tell me, please: what is the point?

_~&_ 24 _&~_

MAKE ME KATE

few years ago I fell in love with a pair of jeans.
More specifically, I fell in love with a pair of jeans
worn by Kate Moss. Designed by UK label Ghost
and dyed a deep shade of indigo, they had a high waist and
large, silver buttons riveted up the front to cinch them in
tight. Little peaks rising to the front and back were perfect
for clipping on a pair of red braces, in a cheeky reference
to the 'rude boy' uniforms of the mod movement. Kate had
paired them with a red and navy silk scarf woven through
the loops, and red suede pumps, in the picture I tore out
from the trashy magazine I was skimming, to store away in
my file of fashion references. The article's intention was
to lament her doomed love affair with suicidally addicted
Pete Doherty, but I only had eyes for the denim. I'd been
looking for those jeans all my life.

I wonder how many others have fallen prey to the same
fate? Amorous affection for an item of clothing you will
never wear as well as a model, and certainly never ever wear
as well as La Moss, that beguiling wisp of a fashion icon.
She is very good at her job, make no mistake about it. I've
been following her enchanted Pied Piper-like conga line

since those first advertisements for Calvin Klein underwear graced every school bus stop in the country. I bought
the cleverly marketed unisex perfume, ck one (hook, line,
and sinker), when I was sixteen. Never mind the undertone
of Aerogard I detected, most effective for treating a case
of the malarial mozzie—it was my first saved-up-for-and-
purchased perfume. I drowned myself in the stuff, trailing
a noxious cloud wherever I went. And I wore my Calvins on
display above the waistband of my jeans for at least one year
hence (a fashion choice I swear I'll never make again). On
top of it all, Kate has personal taste in spades, and always
manages to choose fashion-forward ensembles both on and
off the catwalk, continuously sparking new trends in her
wake. Her look evolves; I think that's what I like the most. I
couldn't give a hoot about her preference for Class-As. And
coat-hanger? *Phooey!* The girl always, always looks good.

Topshop, that behemoth of UK high-street fashion, is
well aware of her unique allure. That's why they got Kate
to design several ranges for them. (And French luxury
leathergoods brand, Longchamp, got in on the act, with
Kate creating a range of handbags for them.) On 1 May
2007, the BBC reported on the near-frenzy in Topshop's
flagship store in London's Oxford Street when Kate
Moss's first-ever range as a designer was released. A grid-
locked flock of fans and die-hard shoppers were treated
to a ten-second glimpse of a kohl-eyed Kate—modelling
a long, strawberry hued frock with several floaty layers
and ruffled sleeves, of her own imagination—in the store
window before the curtains drew closed for the madness to
begin. Inside that window she stood, like some rare exotic

flower with its petals gently falling towards the ground, one hand on her hip in a store dummy pose but eyes smouldering through the glass. Pictures reveal London bobbies roaming the exuberant and youthful crowds, anxious to keep the peace. Because they understood as well as I do: shoppers are lovers, yes, but sometimes they are also fighters.

I scanned the Kate Moss range online with each new season, lamenting the shipping costs from the UK, which

put most items in the costly range of high design, and prefer-
ring to find my fix when I could try things on in the flesh.
One must be brave to brave online shopping overseas when,
naturally, your funds are gobbled up by the postage (and
irretrievable taxes if you need to send it back). Plus, I refused
to pay for cheap synthetics: not necessarily all that Topshop
stocks, but their staple nonetheless. Don't get me wrong, I
love their clever versions of catwalk fashion, but I'm a natural
fibre fetishist. Only when, and if, something comes in 100
per cent cotton, silk or wool, will I look at it twice.

So, rewind to a few years ago and hit pause: here I am with
my ripped-out image, and coming up is a trip to the UK to
visit friends and my beloved in-laws. A quick search online
reveals that the pin-transforming beauties are stocked at my
favourite department store, Liberty of London, so I keep
my fingers crossed they'll have a pair in my size in two weeks'
time, stowing the sartorial inspiration in the front pocket
of my near-empty suitcase, with its space saved for all my
fashion purchases.

Off the plane at Heathrow after a gruelling twenty-
four-hour flight, I bed down for the night at Hamish and
Katie's home in Fulham, before striking off on the Tube in
search of said jeans first thing the next morning.

Finally, I am standing in front of the Ghost concession at Liberty. It's been a long journey. An inquiry to the
helpful sales girl reveals that *yes*, they do have one more
pair in my size. Not in the coveted indigo, mind, but a
more faded version. But they fit like a dream. Oh, joy!
I'm surprised my credit card doesn't show the burn marks
after its quick-draw from my wallet.

They needed dyeing. Easy. But do you think I've got around to it in the past few years? Do you think I've worn those jeans more than once, which was the very day I purchased them? Oh no, I have not. For a start, my thighs and rear end do not bear comparison to Kate's in those jeans, and I damned well knew it when I longingly willed them to look amazing in the tastefully dimmed Liberty change-room. Nor would they, even a few shades darker. High-waisted jeans were unkind to so many the first time around and it seems I did not learn the lesson come their reinvented heyday. Plus, these ones really are unmistakeably high—they finish somewhere between navel and breasts.

Not only that: my husband hates them. Loathes them. Cannot *not* comment every time I so much as fleetingly *think* of wearing them.

'I *hate* you in those jeans—high-waisted doesn't look good on anyone,' he repeatedly asserts.

Oh no, my angel, I think you'll agree they do look good on Kate—but then so would a hessian sack. I can wear them with a long top but what's the point? The buttons look bulky when worn under anything at all—those jeans were made for a bodysuit. And thus, they are completely spoiled for me, forever more.

But I do hold on to them. They're in my bottom drawer, along with seven other pairs of costly jeans that I do not wear, each with their own story to tell, and the one pair of skinny indigo jeans by Lover—a current favourite label— that I actually do wear (not even very often these days, given my current love of frocks). Just waiting until I can harden my heart against them; harden it enough to get rid of them, once and for all. I still have the magazine image of Kate, too, carefully clipped out and stored once again in my folder of fashion inspirations.

Everything about her looked so right on that night as she stepped out of a black cab on her way to some trendy club or bar; her long wavy hair the exact shade of honey, the mix of colours which matched the black biker jacket and tight cotton tee worn up top, the too-cool-for-school lope which spoke of an enviable, enigmatic insouciance. I'm no stalker, Kate, I promise, but it was you I fell in love with for a minute there, not those jeans. Damn you, gossip magazines and fashion in general (you know I don't really mean it). Damn you, stupid brain that went and got tricked again.

Why do we do it to ourselves, time and time again? Something indefinable and elusive works to draw me in, and speaks to me of something else. For all the above reasons, that night her look simply broadcast all that I wished I could say. I'm no different from any lascivious man, really; I get seduced by a well-turned heel and mysterious air. But I don't want to acquire the object of my affections—I want to climb inside her life and become her, just for a little while. Usually when all else fails.

Treacherously needy thoughts like these always seem to be accompanied by a fallow period. A time when I'm feeling less than myself, or less than lots of things. For a time there—the time of my most recent Kate obsession—it didn't seem much was working. My career felt a bit non-existent, I was creatively frustrated and we couldn't afford the down-payment on a home when everyone around me seemed to be steadily marching towards their own brighter futures. I projected all my desires onto those jeans, and a model; the very epitome of all that is unobtainable. Somehow thinking that if I could just look like that, things would improve.

It's been a while since I got so seduced by an image. My Kate fetish has worn off, no doubt to be revived again sometime in the future. But I have learned something: you can't steal someone's style, not really—any more than you can be someone else. You can mimic it, but you'll never look as good unless you find one of your own. It's no more possible than finding life happiness by attempting to mirror the exact formula of someone else's. Such a simple observation, yes, but one it's taken me so foolishly long to understand.

And now I have to admit to another affection, for pop songstress Lily Allen. I like Lily. She seems like a real girl. A fabulously rich, multi-million-album-selling success, yes—but a real girl, nonetheless, potty mouth and all. The girl's got charisma. Her saccharine melodies with bite are not unlike Kate's talent for wearing anything humdrum with edge. And she's even better live in concert, I found, when I saw her perform a few years ago. I should've taken her cue when she sang ironically, 'If I wear those jeans, I can look like Kate Moss', but I didn't, more fool me. At least it proves one thing though: at the end of it all, I'm not alone.

A note on choosing the most delectable denims ... Clearly I'm no expert, but I have learned some things over the years. My top tip for lasting jeans success is weight; those beauties need to be *thick,* but with a very small amount of give just to suck you in that bit further. But no straining at the seams. That looks cheap. No, I never said it was easy.

Boyfriend jeans are wonderful for some. On me, they evoke the look of a scruffy house-painter. But maybe I'm not thinking fashion-forward enough. Fitted is, generally, best.

If you really don't like yourself in jeans, consider ditching them altogether in favour of a skirt or frock. Yes, jeans are a wardrobe staple, but they're fickle friends. They're the first to betray you when the going gets tough: you stop exercising, you forget which style is in, or the muffins give you a muffin-top.

Don't wash your denims with fabric softener. I use it on everything else, but not my precious jeans. They get all slouchy in no time at all and you'll ruin them if you're a sucker for washing after every wear. As for darker colours (which really are the best for their slimming properties), they need to go through the wash inside out if you want to keep the colour true. You could even throw a cup of salt in there with them once in a while, just to lock it down.

I shall tell you a funny thing that my lovely friend Trevor Bell told me recently. He says, don't wash your jeans—pop them in the freezer! It kills all the germs, and you don't have to worry about them losing their colour. The only tricky thing is explaining what the hell they're doing in there to friends during dinner parties, when someone inevitably goes searching for the ice to top up a G&T.

~ 25 ~

HAND-ME-DOWNS

I have never really been much of a hoarder. Given the opportunity, I think I could have been, but I've moved so often over the past three decades to different homes, cities and countries that I've simply learned over time to divest myself of unnecessary things. While I hold onto a few favourite letters and books, I can be quite ruthless when it comes to clothes. If I haven't worn something for a while, I often gift pieces to friends who I think might get some use out of them. Or I carefully fold and send them packing to a local charity store, or hold a stall at a flea market with my closest girlfriends so we can recycle, recoup a little money, and enjoy a fun day together in the process.

I like to see my old frocks walk away with new people; someone who might appreciate and adore them afresh, breathe new life into their pre-worn threads and weave their own stories into the tale of those inanimate objects I once loved. I find it particularly pleasing to see women in their teens and twenties alight on an item I no longer fit into, or that doesn't suit my current lifestyle, and find something in it to treasure when it flatters them the way it once did me. When I see a friend (or, on some occasions, a stranger) walking around in a piece I recognise as something that was once mine, it gives me a little thrill to know that clothes, too, have a life of their own to lead.

But now that I have a daughter, I've begun to think about the things I might like to keep for her sake; items she might be able to enjoy when she grows older. For me, clothes are the most potent bearers of my memories. I have an almost encyclopaedic recall for the items I wore on different occasions, or when something momentous occurred in my life. Even just for the phases or feelings I was going through at certain times, when I spy something that jogs both the little and large events of my history. A pattern or colour on fabric can conjure up so many emotions, just as surely as a scent or a song or a remembered phrase can. Whether my clothes will actually be worth anything or not in time is neither here nor there, but I'd like them to be somehow valuable, because she knows I once cherished them, or because they remind her of happy events in her own past.

Fifteen years is a long time to wait, because that's how long it will be before she's even old enough to possibly wear them. By then I have a feeling we will have moved again, maybe several times, and the urge to purge might be too great. And who knows if she'll hate them, or think they're badly dated or even ugly; or be too embarrassed by me to remotely consider trotting out in anything that was once mine? Or will she dream of the time she is set to inherit them, and relish adding her own stories to their particular tale? Will she covet some of my pieces, and beg to borrow them, and prize them dearly when they in time become her own? I can't possibly know. But I have a feeling I'll be weak-willed when it comes to anything she likes—my mother was the same. I will let her have it, even if I adore it myself, because I'll be proud to have chosen something she thinks worthy of her attention.

Casting my mind back to favourite outfits I have worn over the years, I can certainly remember a few I would journey back in time to pluck from their fate and instead save for her. Such as the black and gold evening gown paired with strappy suede platform heels, worn to a formal dinner and dance I attended towards the end of school.

I was in Grade 11, but a Grade 12 boy—Billy Marsh—had invited me as his guest to the Leavers' Dinner. He was a really nice boy, Billy, and I rather regret leaving him alone for most of the evening (preoccupied as I was with another boy on the other side of the room). Of all my photos, I treasure the ones from that evening. One image, taken with two lost friends, shows us standing in front of the white, open-topped Cadillac we journeyed in to the stately home where the event was to be held. I am standing between them, arms slung happily over their shoulders, and grinning from ear to ear. I'm leaning back slightly, hips tilted sideways against the door of the car, and I look bubbly and cheeky and so very convinced of my place in the world. I think, possibly, that I thought I knew everything that night. How funny that I should be convinced of the very opposite thing a full seventeen years later.

Another reason I love the memory of that dress is because of its provenance. When I was fifteen, I spent some time during my school holidays working at the factory for Studibaker Hawk, a fashion label created by designer Janelle Smith, artist Wendy Arnold and architect David Miles.

Studibaker's heyday was back in the 1980s, with some of its frocks featured in both Sydney's Powerhouse Museum and the National Gallery of Victoria; so indicative are they of the entire decade. But back then I simply knew they specialised in formal and wedding dresses, and spent many hot, hazy days in the high-ceilinged warehouse wading through racks and racks of dresses from each collection, looking over each one carefully for any flaws, and snipping off the many loose threads poking out from perfect seams. When finished with each one, I applied a sticker to the label reading QC, followed by a number, to show where I'd been. I was paid something like five dollars an hour, and I remember listening to mix tapes on my Sony Walkman as I worked; Talking Heads, Crowded House, and Huey Lewis and The News. Glamour couldn't have been further from my mind.

In 1992, I bought that black and gold dress at Studibaker's annual clearance sale for far less than it was worth, and saved it for a full year before I had the opportunity to wear it. It was a perfect size 10, its fit precise with its lovely gold lamé halter-neck bodice (lined to stop it from being scratchy) and long black ankle-length skirt. It had a slit up its left side which swayed open, a little suggestively, as I walked. At the back it had a single invisible zip down the spine, and its only other embellishment was a black satin band circling the bodice at its empire line.

I wish I had saved it for Olive's own first formal, or even for her to play dress-ups in; it was significantly less revealing than the frocks I've seen other young girls wearing out on the town. I would tell her the story of that steamy summer in a rag trade warehouse, and maybe hint at the evening I went on to have in it, but sadly I've no idea where it is now. Of course, I'm not really longing for it with her in mind, but for more selfish reasons; maybe trying to recapture something of that era, and the bygone me.

Another long lost love is the fifties playsuit I unearthed in a charity store, somewhere on the outskirts of Melbourne, when I was nineteen. Canary yellow cotton with a black and white geometric design, it had a shirred back and stiff conical cups which made me feel like a Varga pin-up. I wore it every second day throughout the heatwave of that summer, with cork wedges and a pair of cat's eye sunglasses, washing it carefully by hand in the bathroom sink of the student digs I shared with a bunch of other misfits, lest it be destroyed by our temperamental washing machine. And I sunbathed in it, lazily reading trashy novels and fashion magazines in the unkempt back-yard, procrastinating over the writing of yet another overdue essay. I can imagine telling Olive about my unruly housemates, and how I wish I had studied a little harder, for we never really appreciate the opportu-nities we have in life until they're gone. Perhaps she would have laughed, and tried it on just to please me. Or worn it out one brave night, with a white shirt tied just under those crazy cups (as I once did).

I do have at least one piece put aside for her. A silk dress, just a wisp of a thing really, cut on the bias and layered with a sea foam chiffon and Japanese dotted flower print, it has a pale blue slip underneath and deliberately frayed, ruffled flower at the left shoulder of its twisted silk straps. The hem falls prettily to the ankles, and it floats around the body in a dreamy fashion, looking beautiful with softly loosened curls and silver sandals, and a single, silver charm on a thin necklace.

It was my 'wedding' dress; rather, the dress I wore to many weddings, when I lived in London and had one to attend every other weekend for a time. James bought it for me after he asked me to accompany him as his plus one, on the first of many such invitations. We'd only been going out for a few months, but he took me to a chic little Richmond boutique to shop for it. It had been a perfect August day, spent cycling and basking in the sunlight of an atmospheric beer garden near the park during lunch. Being poorer than a church mouse at that time, I gasped involuntarily at the price tag, but he swept it off to the counter for me, and I felt properly spoiled. It was the first time a man ever bought me anything to wear, and it confirmed my suspicions that he was a keeper.

I've not worn that dress for more than five years now, because it feels dated, formal and a bit frou-frou, and I can't think of a place to wear it to. I've been to weddings since, but it never seemed right for the occasion given that people tend to don cocktail dress to celebrate a marriage in Australia, and not the floral silk sheaths so popular at English country weddings. But maybe one day Olive will find the place and the time where it looks fresh again. For now it sits, gently folded between sheets of acid-free tissue paper, in a box on the top of her wardrobe, beneath a sachet of lavender sprigs. Waiting, just waiting.

~ 26 ~

SWIMMING WITH SHARKS

ais oui, there are clothes for myriad occasions. There are clothes to wear when you meet sharky people. You know the kind: sharp, calculating, carnivorous. They give you a sense of unease in their presence. When you're dealing with these kinds of people, you only have two (fashion) options.

Option one: look sharky yourself. Kit yourself out in that power suit with Balmain shoulders. Show them you're a force to be reckoned with. Utilise your clothes to say, I'm not afraid of you. This can be particularly useful when dealing with all sorts of dodgy types; people who appreciate the power of front. If they think you're another predator, they might steer clear. Then again, you could end up mauling each other to death.

Option two, the far more subtle choice: appear demure. Weak, even. Wear a floaty sundress; step back from the challenge, take yourself out of the equation. You might be mistaken for foolish; in fact, it's highly likely you will. Take it all in. Softly, softly. Catch more flies with honey. Live to fight another day.

27

DRESSING FOR TWO

Before I fell pregnant (such an odd euphemism, as though one has simply slipped and found themselves in this new state; the other less delicate but more adequate description being 'knocked up'), I largely romanticised the fertile womanly figure. Even those poor unfortunate ladies who looked all puffed up and bloated, waddling along in the last trimester, fascinated me with their globe-shaped girth which spoke of such possibility. I often imagined how I would clothe my own pregnant body one day.

Initially lovely to me were the hippies I spied in Byron Bay as a teenager, or on remote Thai beaches later on. Wearing cropped cheesecloth tops and tie-dyed sarongs, those leather-sandalled, dreadlocked maidens paraded their nut-brown bellies with a swaying walk. They'd often have a few small children behind them, dutifully following after their mother. Beads and woven leather straps were wrapped casually around their necks and a small stud usually glinted in the nose; maybe a piece or two of tattooed body art was on display. Such pagan beauty, I thought. They looked so wonderful, and so very right in their stretched-taut skin. I could easily imagine them as goddesses transported back many centuries ago to some remote island, sporting much the same thing—perhaps an animal skin or two slung over the shoulder the only addition to their earthy charm.

I also admired those who were brave enough to wear stocking-like dresses, making their bumps appear as a snake-ish lunch on an otherwise sleek figure. City-dwelling professional types who, to see the back of them, looked unremarkable, then, turning side-on, revealed a well-rounded tum, hand protectively cupped beneath, plump, flushed faces the picture of health as they waited for the lights to change at a busy street corner. They looked incredibly beautiful to me—so womanly and ripe in such bland urban settings.

Attention-diverting bows and large, shapeless garments never seem to fulfil their potential for the pregnant figure. I think some suppose they can hide beneath them, but I remain unconvinced. I remember colleagues from my days living in Hong Kong who, in the latter stages of their pregnancies, wore tent-like numbers which made them look like overgrown children. Sickly pastel pink or blue frocks edged with white broderie anglaise collars and endless layers of ruffles and frills falling almost to the ground, intended to conceal the wholly obvious and convey a wholesome, virtuous appearance. Confectionery monstrosities, they gave me toothache just to look at them. I quietly wished they would realise they were fooling no-one.

Over the years, thoughts of the kind of pregnant woman I wanted to be when the time came preoccupied me far more than ideas of my perfect wedding. One event you merely experience for the day, the other represents nine months of abundant expectation.

I found out I was pregnant in the very early stages, less than five weeks in. We had lunch arranged at a friend's beachside home over the summer holidays and for the whole journey there and back—indeed, throughout the entire lunch—I felt seasick, the offer of juice mixed with champagne upon arrival making my stomach lurch queasily and the unappetising nature of all food surely indicating something was up. On the way home we stopped in at a chemist and bought a pregnancy kit, and quickly after confirmed our suspicions.

For the entire first twelve weeks of my pregnancy the nauseous feeling increased, before suddenly dissipating overnight. Throughout this time I felt myself become more mentally internal, and less focused on what was going on around me. The much-talked-about baby brain materialised overnight as each thought travelled to me on a slow train, carefully wrapped in cotton wool. Dressing became only one small hurdle in what felt like a series of endless, exhausting tasks each morning. I wanted to curl up in a ball and escape the world instead, clad only in my pyjamas.

It felt such an odd thing to announce I was pregnant. The wholly private act committed with my husband suddenly felt like the subtext I was carrying around with me everywhere. Whether people think it or not when they see you, I certainly felt as though I had a statement emblazoned across my forehead (or, more appropriately, my belly): *I have sex.* That we all do, or wish we do, somehow didn't reassure me in my highly sensitised state. I felt fragile enough as it was. I'm no prude, but in those first few months I felt all awkward and kinky and embarrassed by the

erotic side of my nature, being that it was now so obviously on display (and also, curiously, quite sexy). It seemed a bit inappropriate; I was going to be a mother! Sexiness would not do at all, would it?

In between bouts of morning sickness—'morning' being a gross lie when it happens throughout the entire day and night—I kept visiting sample sales and favourite shopping haunts, on the prowl for new clothes to adorn my pregnant figure once I had a bump to speak of. On reflection, this was a rookie's mistake; in the early stages you've no idea how large you are going to get, and the fit is just as important—if not more so—when you're careening about, ready to burst. You literally can't buy for any other stage than the one you're in, and in no time at all you pass that juncture, too. So it's not as fun as it should be, buying all those new clothes for your burgeoning baby body. You either acquire some things you can never quite fit into, or other items you're able to wear for precisely three seconds before they refuse to shimmy over newly inflated thighs.

At the cutely named One Fish Two Fish I found a pair of Egg Maternity jeans which were nothing short of perfection at three months. Blue-black stretch denim, they had an elasticated waistband above spare, clever stitching which gave the appearance of a non-existent covered zip and back pockets. The lack of adornment was important, because they didn't add any bulk where bulk was not needed, and they had a fitted waist and legs with a straight cut that ended exactly at the ankle; excellent for wearing with flat-soled sandals and a lightly billowing, embroidered white linen peasant blouse. I could just about fool people there wasn't anything hiding underneath—important when I was still keeping the news a secret before passing the milestone of twelve weeks. I wore them for less than a month before the bones of my hips started their steady progress outwards to cradle the baby's girth within; they eventually no longer fit without the help of a shoe horn to lever me in. Soon they didn't fit at all. I put on a whopping twenty kilos in the end, and the next time I fit into those jeans, I had already had Olive months previously.

I tried those other stretchy elastic thingummies you attach to your non-maternity jeans, a small square of fabric meant to conceal your knickers beneath, but my jeans made their way determinedly down my hips in minutes and left me all flustered when I had to keep hitching them up again on the sly. So I gave up on jeans altogether and opted for frocks from the fourth month onwards, which were comfortable and forgiving when I felt more bloated than taut.

Those early months are the hardest to dress for; even if you're lucky enough not to feel ill, you look more like someone who's developed a sudden preoccupation with pies than having the excuse of being in the baby way. It's not until the fourth or fifth month you start to feel your belly's carriage swell directly out in front of you, rather than sitting like a spare tyre or two, unflatteringly wrapped around the middle.

And breasts! I despaired of ways to dress them. It came as a bit of a shock to realise they were actually intended for something other than feminine allure—*what, these things?* My already ample bust swelled by a couple of cup sizes by week six, and then further still as my pregnancy progressed, making me run for re-fittings at a local lingerie store not once but thrice. For women with a small bust who have always wished to be bigger, it must be a nice experience to suddenly wake up one day in possession of such a fulsome cleavage. For me, it was simply bothersome. I longed to wrap and bandage mine down, and largely pretend they didn't exist. For a start, nothing fit my top half properly, even if it did cover the rest of me. Secondly, they felt bruised and sore, like I'd been given a swift punch (*one, two!*) to either side of my chest. Showing them off wasn't an option—I felt slightly obscene. While frocks would look simply gorgeous around the belly and thighs, upper seams stretched taut and ruined the fall of the whole design. My solution was to shelve much of my pre-pregnancy wardrobe and work with a few failsafe pieces in a number of variations instead. Stretchy dresses and separates became my new best friends, as previously coquettish tops were rendered utterly pornographic.

For parties, which I did not say die to until at least the eighth month, I swapped my sensible flats for heeled knee-high boots, but was only able to get away with them for a few hours before my lower back started to throb painfully. In my fifth month, and while attending the Sydney Writers' Festival opening night party, I went several steps too far, and flitted about for many hours in towering, buckled ankle boots because I so missed wearing them. After which I was effectively hobbled for days, my back protesting from the minute I rolled, with momentum, out of bed each morning.

Towards the end, my staples became the fifties wrap-around skirts, stretch tops and shrunken cardigans which I ended up wearing long into the months after the birth, and still wear on occasion. I wore my favourite black skirt, a

1950s vintage number festooned with bunches of overblown red roses, wrapped tightly just beneath my belly, with a simple stretch merino wool top with three-quarter-length sleeves and scooped neckline. (Now I simply wear the skirt higher around my waist, such is the adaptability of the endlessly clever wraparound skirt!) If it was cold, I popped on a woollen beanie or scarf and fur-lined boots and, if not, I pared back to slip-on shoes and a simple necklace or beads to complete the look. Once my belly became so huge I felt I wasn't just pretending (more than merely bloated, as it seemed in those first few months), I loved to show it off with clothes that cosseted and enhanced my feeling of being womanly and ripe. Before then, it was simply difficult, and looking stylish *and* preggers proved surprisingly challenging.

I remember my neighbour Emily, who was pregnant at the same time as me (her boy, Harvey, was born a few short months after Olive), walking down our local main street the day she gave birth. It was hot, the very beginning of summer, and she wore a V-neck T-shirt tightly fitted over her massive belly, with a batik wraparound skirt that was not quite able to meet her top. A wide-brimmed floppy hat covered her brown bob, and curly haired Ruby, all of three, wandered beside her as they walked past Olive and me as we sat outside the Last Drop Café sharing a pot of tea with a friend. I watched Emily plant each foot slowly in front of the other; she looked nothing short of magnificent. That night, Emily gave birth at home, and the next morning as we were leaving the house the whole family came out onto the lawn to greet us, new babe in arms and Emily clad in a green cotton dressing gown splashed with a soft pink and apple green paisley print. Weary, relieved and glowing; I remember thinking she was the very picture of worship-able female beauty.

I haven't lost my admiration for pregnant women even now I've been one, although the mystery is gone. I still think they look almost unbearably beautiful, and regal, even in those last stages when they seem to glide carefully along, bodies large ships and bellies prow-like, parting crowds like the sea. They *are* romantic; full of the wonder of new life for that fleeting time before they sink back into the sea of ordinariness, and the daily task of simply living. When we're pregnant, we resemble so much more the animals that we are.

Nowadays my body is the least attractive in the flesh that it's ever been, with the stories of childbirth and nursing writ large across it. I've stretch marks where once there were none. My belly is no longer flat, because for nine months I forgot how to hold my stomach muscles in (a wholly unnatural pose when you're pregnant; I've gone and lost the knack). And lately, I've traded exercise for writing time and time with Olive, so all my body's tone has flown out the window. But to be honest, I don't really see its flaws, or castigate myself for them even half as much as I once did. I'm more forgiving of my body, and more appreciative of others'. *It works,* that's what I think when I look at the reflection staring back at me in the mirror. It grew a life inside it, so more than anything, I feel proud. For the first time, I actually love it—even if I never look the same in jeans again.

My recommendations for good pregnancy wear are this: Stretchy cotton or wool frocks (depending upon the season) in as tight a fit as you feel comfortable in; those that land above the knee if you are happy to show off your legs, or further down if you don't love your calves. They will make you feel less frumpy than the looser kind of dress.

Stretchy tops, for the very same reason.

A shrunken woollen cardi, prettily decorated pashmina, scarf or fur gilet. This should be enough to keep you warm when it's cold out, because your body becomes so hot and heavy with all that extra blood being pumped around. (I rarely needed a coat or anything extra to keep me from my customary near-freezing state.)

A fabulous wraparound skirt or two. These skirts will be your friends, long after your baby is out, rather than in.

Excellent hipster or maternity tights, depending on the season. (I was most heavily pregnant throughout winter; for summer you can simply go bare-legged.) My favourites were the footless kind edged with lace at the ankle, sporting a rounded section to pull up over your belly, or tuck neatly beneath. As long as they don't creep down—there's nothing worse.

Pretty, comfy flats such as ballet slippers or strappy leather sandals. Give the heels a miss for anything but special occasions. Trust me on this, and your back will forever thank you for it.

(These suggestions suit an office environment, but you can work through variations on this theme around the clock, no matter where you go.)

——◦ 28 ◦——

HOMEMADE HAPPINESS

I have a habit—a hobby, if you will—which up until a few years ago was seen to be deeply uncool.

I craft.

Yes, that's right, I like to make things. Not arty, edgy things—the likes of which you might see in a Museum of Contemporary Art or Tate Modern exhibition. Just homely, pretty items that I use every day, such as cloth shopper bags and rag rugs and hot water bottle covers to keep me warm in winter. And I'm not even in my seventies. What's more, I've been doing it for years now; ever since I was a young girl. But it's only recently that I've begun to admit to it with a degree of pride because, you see, craft is suddenly hip again.

As a child and then a teenager, I was always enthusiastic to try new things, but was quite an impatient and restless soul. I dabbled in so many pastimes, from playing guitar to scuba diving, and ballet dancing to singing—even planting trees with a weekend green group and (to the mirth of everyone who knows me) modelling. Few of the things I dabbled in stuck, but sewing's one of them and it's born out of my lifelong love of, and interest in, fashion.

Given the lucky country and generation I grew up in, it's no surprise that I'm a terrible consumerist; always wanting new things. But I didn't have the money for designer clothes as a teenager, and the modelling career never took off, so, naturally, I didn't get all the perks, the free stuff which largely inspired me to become a model in the first place (along with the desire, if I'm honest, to be told I was beautiful—but don't all young girls want that?). That's when I started customising fashion or, more to the point, the unloved items which ended up in my local charity store; altering these pieces to resemble more closely the highly desirable items I saw in magazines.

Deftness with a needle and thread certainly came in handy when I wanted to shorten the hemline of a heavily embellished sixties kaftan, or decorate the lapels of an old man's tweed coat, to be worn with a black shift, chunky Doc Martens and heavily teased fringe to a much-anticipated underage disco. It also helped when my fellow Catholic school friends and I discovered how much extra attention one could gain from members of the opposite sex at the neighbouring boys' college when we hitched up our positively Victorian skirts by a few inches. Sometimes we went too far and the nuns noticed the staples or masking tape we'd used as a temporary measure, earning us a stern talking-to and an afternoon's detention. The ability to hide our treachery with small, professional stitches—swearing blind that we'd grown overnight—proved a godsend in that situation (although I'm not sure He would agree).

For many years, the sole crafting I indulged in involved dyeing pale lace underwear (that I'd accidentally turned a grubby shade of grey in the wash) to a fabulous shocking pink or electric blue, and chopping bits off voluminous eighties cast-offs to better suit the times and show off my slim, adolescent figure. I turned floor-length 1970s silk evening gowns into Twiggy-esque numbers, and repaired painstakingly hand-beaded, holey cardigans (which had had one too many run-ins with cashmere-loving moths) into good-as-new beauties. I covered stains with clever patches of floral fabric, and re-purposed lovely peacock-hued saris which still bore the faint smell of musk-scented incense from their days on the subcontinent as curtains in various student digs. I hid my sewing skills in my mid-teens, mainly because I didn't want to admit that so many of the clothes I wore were not brand new.

Later, vintage became popular and I wore my odd, salvaged crinolines and mended taffeta skirts with pride, paired with tiny boleros (after the grid-iron shoulder pads had been snipped out) and numerous silk flowers pinned liberally throughout my hair. But I kept customising, for most of the items I wore had usually been discarded for a reason and, truth be told, I enjoyed it.

Later still, as my career as a publicist took me all over the world, any disposable income I had tended to be spent on holidays I tacked on to the end of business trips in such far-flung destinations as Shanghai, São Paulo, Bangkok or Munich, as well as dining and dancing into the wee hours like the committed hedonist I was. Throughout this time, I continued to modify opportunity shop discards and rummage gleefully in the charity stores and flea markets I sought out, from Tasmania to the north of Scotland, from New York's East Village to Istanbul's Grand Bazaar, idly daydreaming of all the heady sights my clothes had seen.

When, at the age of twenty-seven, I got married and settled down somewhat, I channelled my passions into becoming a number one, bona-fide Suzy Homemaker. Previously an exuberant (but rather untalented) cook, I bought a copy of Nigella Lawson's *How to Be a Domestic Goddess*, threw elaborate, rowdy dinner parties for friends and whiled away weekends reading interiors magazines or browsing through homewares stores like any other smug married. I kept tabs on affordable art, and purchased a statement piece or two of furniture.

Then, in 2007, James and I bought our first home together, a Victorian cottage in the city's inner suburbs, and the happy acquisition of new things drew firmly to a halt as our mortgage gobbled up all our disposable income.

It sounds incredibly dull, but for one whole year we documented every dollar we spent. During the process, we did the maths and realised we frittered away literally thousands each year on gifts. Think about it: a few weddings here, a baby shower there and birthdays aplenty ... it all adds up. Especially when you leave it to the last minute, panic, and run into the nearest store on your way to a party. We didn't want to stop buying presents for friends so thought instead, *How can we be more canny with our cash?* We decided that making—rather than buying—some of our gifts was one solution.

And that's when I *really* started crafting, and not just pre-loved clothes. I began making cute, whimsical things for friends and their children. Tentative at first, I soon threw myself into it when my one-offs elicited a genuinely enthusiastic response. I embellished tiny vests and made soft toys from old jumpers for new babies, as well as brightly patterned summer beach bags and floaty cotton tops, homewares and accessories of all sorts, and hand-decorated cards and wrapping paper. I sourced vintage and remnant items I knew my friends would appreciate, or fashioned them into something I knew they didn't have or could put to use, always making sure I had them in mind while I stitched or painted. It often took less time to craft something than a shopping trip would have taken. With a linen cupboard full of deliciously soft old jumpers that had seen better days, or fabric and ribbons that caught my eye, as well as a minimal sewing kit, I had all the ingredients I needed for constructing gifts anytime—even half an hour before I was due somewhere.

In addition to that, our old-new home inspired me. We simply could not afford all the designer items we wanted, so I turned my hand to making them myself and created all sorts of things, from paintings and collages on canvas to fill the walls, to cosy lamb's wool throws and cushions made with gorgeous Fornasetti fabric for the sofa. I taught myself to renovate sombre, tired furniture with milk paint and beeswax, and covered chairs and lampshades with luscious remnants. I discovered that necessity is indeed the mother of invention, and felt intensely happy surrounding us with things we had made or reconditioned ourselves. I bought a slew of craft and decoration books for inspiration but discovered I have a kind of dyslexia when it comes to reading patterns. So I attempted making things in my own trial-and-error way, *sans* instructions. They still turned out beautifully ... most of the time.

When I visited the new wave of fabric and craft supplies stores popping up all over town, I met other young women— from film-makers, artists and mothers to bankers and company directors—who had, like me, discovered just how satisfying it is to make things by hand, particularly in a time when so many of our purchases are constructed in a factory. Forging new friendships over morning or afternoon tea, I found these women had been driven to crafting by the beautiful range of materials on offer, as well as tighter and tighter budgets as the financial crisis hit. While a lampshade can cost up to several hundred dollars in a store, making one yourself (even with the most expensive, fashionable fabrics) still only costs a fraction of that price. And making it yourself means it is exactly what you want, rather than a compromise as so many items we buy often are.

I can trace my first non-clothing-related sewing adventure back to buying a length of divine Florence Broadhurst 'running horses' fabric in a sale and thinking, *What to make?*—before turning it into a simple weekend shopper bag. Similarly, my clever friend Rebecca—a writer, social researcher and director of a company—whiles away the evening

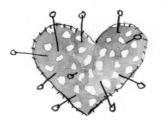

hours with her husband, small daughter, a few balls of baby alpaca wool and her knitting needles for company. Another producer friend—a gorgeous, girl-about-town type—gets a kick out of making insanely difficult knits (the likes of which you might see on a model sashaying down the runway for Comme des Garçons or Yohji Yamamoto), and made the most divine scarf for her boyfriend's birthday from the softest merino wool she'd ever come across.

Since I've started crafting, I've been amazed by the beautiful, inspiring things I've been introduced to on an almost daily basis. Crafters are prodigious bloggers, and are more than happy to share new finds with each other (check out excellent blogs such as Jane Brocket's Yarnstorm, Posie Gets Cozy, and Six and a Half Stitches if you don't believe me; or heavily craft-influenced design sites such as Design*Sponge and Decor8). These sites feature items that are no more redolent of your beloved gran's creations than the chic items you'll find in an upmarket boutique. I'm also grateful for the new people craft has brought into my life. I've become so passionate, I even wrote a book about it, *The Crafty Minx,* and maintain a blog which keeps me constantly interacting with other crafters.

When time is a commodity we value more highly than any other, spending it on someone you care about really resonates; far more than a voucher to their favourite store. But most of all, I've found it intensely satisfying to indulge in the sense of calm that stitching up a storm seems to bring, and in surrounding myself and my family with these special, handmade items. For me, at least, it's where happiness lies.

_29_

BRAVE NEW LOOK

Our daughter, Olive Rose Doust, was born on 8 September, 2008, at 2.11 pm. We arrived at the hospital, well-rested under the circumstances, at about 7.30 am, ready and waiting for me to be induced. The induction—the breaking of my waters and a shot of the drug oxytocin to stimulate contractions—took place just before 9 am. A mere five-and-a-bit hours later, Olive appeared, hollering and blue. Up until that point, that had been me in my hospital gown, similarly noisy and clothed in almost the same violet-tinged shade.

I had an easy pregnancy, and an easy birth, all things considered. The final few weeks had been spent lying down on the sofa or in bed, because I developed a torn ligament which meant my back was in agony. The pain was draining—I was so sick of being big. Having carried 14 extra kilos throughout the majority of the pregnancy, I stacked on a further six in those final weeks before the birth, just from the inactivity and being a bit maudlin. I found comfort in food, drinking endless cups of decaffeinated tea and steadily munching my way through packets of biscuits and large bowls of pasta. But apart from that, and some tiredness, the time passed by in a hazy dream.

It is no wonder that I hurt my back—I was entirely to blame. There is a picture of me, at more than eight months pregnant, wearing paint-splattered black yoga pants and a wraparound cream cashmere jumper, very old and holey. Underneath, a grey marle singlet, riding up to show my neat, rounded belly, *linea nigra* visible and snaking down towards the top of my cotton-lycra trousers. I am perched precariously on the edge of the bathtub in our tiny wash-room, a few feet up from the ground, hair in a hastily pulled up bun and wisps escaping around my face, a white-dipped paint brush in right hand. I am grinning into the camera lens, a little ruefully.

Passing by the bathroom door, James had thought it hilarious to find me hell bent on painting the ceiling at this late stage of my pregnancy. After taking my picture he asked:

'So, do you think you might, just possibly, be doing that thing ... Nesting?'

'Nope,' I replied. 'Whatever do you mean?'

But I followed the painting that afternoon with a full dusting of the skirting boards, a vehement working at old stains on the kitchen floor, and a scrubbing of all the windows in an early, diligent spring clean.

Then, two days after that, I was driving home from lunch with a friend and passed the gardening centre up the road. They had several flowering magnolia trees, each about six feet tall, displayed on the footpath outside the gates. I backed up and parked the car out the front, nego-tiating my way out of the driver's seat. I was wearing my stretchy silk-jersey Luella dress, the one with the black and white stripes and mirrored Perspex buttons down the front, which looked far better now I was pregnant, being that it was tight and fitted and showed my bump off to its full potential (rather than an untoned tummy and VPL). On my feet I wore a much-loved pair of leather indigo boots with low Cuban heels over grey opaque tights. Smudged kohl was around my eyes, unfocused through lack of sleep. My hair was blow-dried straight and arranged in an aurora around my head, far fuller and thicker in pregnancy than it usually looked. Just the day before, as I was wheeling the rubbish bins out for collection, a group of kids from the local high school had been walking past and I heard one of them mutter something about Aslan (the lion from C.S. Lewis' *The Lion, the Witch and the Wardrobe*) under his breath. I had hoped, at least, that he thought I couldn't hear.

I carefully inspected the trees, which were just what I'd been looking for to replace the dead fern currently proving an eyesore in a large terracotta pot on stone blocks just outside our kitchen window. I bought the plant with the most flowers, along with two 10 kilogram bags of soil to plant it in, and managed to manoeuvre it into the passenger door of our sedan, all the while dismissing the proffered help of the concerned-looking sales assistant.

Arriving home, the thought struck me that I could leave the tree and the bags of dirt in the car until James arrived home, for him to ferry inside and out the back. I was concerned about not messing up my frock, more than anything. Then I decided, *I'll be fine, I'll just carry them held out from my body to avoid ruining the dress.* I really wanted to get that tree planted, pronto. Why the urgency? I can't tell you.

So I proceeded to cart each item into the house, down our long hallway, through the living room and the kitchen and out to the garden, shedding clods of soil and bark chips along the way and huffing a bit as I did, careful only not to trip.

I retraced my steps to sweep the wooden floors, bending down with difficulty over my pregnant stomach to collect the mess into a brush and pan, almost toppling over more than once. Then, I changed into the yoga pants and a long-sleeve cotton top, plus a pair of old ugg boots, before violently ripping out the dying fern, replacing it with the magnolia, pouring in the soil, and patting it down. At the last bend to tamp down the bulging soil around the maze of roots, I felt something twinge in my lower back. Uh-oh. When I stood up, a searing pain shot up to my shoulder and down my left leg. A band of ache formed, throbbing like a bruise around my hips, causing me to promptly sit down on the cement floor, to have a little pant, and a think. I might have stayed there a while.

That night, we went to see David Sedaris talk at the Opera House; he was in town promoting his latest book. I'd had tickets for months and was not about to miss out, sore back or no, and dosed up on tablets to ease the pain. For two hours we sat in the theatre with me shifting uncomfortably, having difficulty with each new position in finding any relief. Laughter helped, but then it didn't, as every action made it worse and I tried to stop, holding my sides as I did. One look sideways at James' face and I was in mirthful agony. As we exited the building, I was limping; into a cab and then home, where I was totally unable to fall asleep.

My back still gives me trouble. Even now, a full eighteen months later, and even though I'm carrying less weight than I did before I fell pregnant. But it's not something I often think about, unless I bend to pick up Olive without thinking, or stupidly load myself up with more grocery shopping than is sensible, with her still hoisted on my hip.

The pain seems such a small price to pay, in exchange. Our wee girl is bonny, and sweet—a happy baby, except for when she is not. Cheeky, noisy and wilful, she looks like James, and a bit like me.

I remember the thrill of excitement when, five months after giving birth and warily avoiding the scales previously, I weighed myself for the first time in ages only to find I had lost all the extra weight I had gained, and a few kilos extra besides. I have breastfeeding a hungry baby to thank. And the running around in circles, between changing and writing and feeding and cooking and popping on endless cycles of washing each day as I did. It was such a joy to pull down all those carefully stored boxes of pre-pregnancy clothes from the top of the wardrobe, and to sift through them again, reliving memories of the last time I wore them and trying on everything to see how it fit.

The room was covered in piles of discarded clothing when I finished, hastily flung over an armchair or on the bed and over a hanging rack with my imperative to get through all those things. To be honest, I hadn't expected to come near many of them ever again. I felt like a kid in a candy store with a sweet tooth and a bulging purse of spare change, surrounded by lollies laid out before me that had for so long been kept out of reach. My old clothes felt new again.

Nowadays, I'm wider in the hips and thighs and have a larger behind than before; the optical illusion means I now look slimmer in the waist—go figure. And my bust has dropped a cup size, a welcome change, meaning I'm more of a pear-shape than I used to be when I was all top-heavy and slim legs. With my love of 1950s-inspired styling and admiration for the Dior New Look shape, this suits me perfectly.

Some items I was holding on to no longer worked and had to be culled, so I folded them and considered where they could be re-homed. Mostly, those no-longer-appropriate pieces consisted of items I didn't want any more anyway: woollen trousers initially bought for wintery work days in the office; some frocks which were verging on the too tightly fitted beforehand. A couple of bustiers, too—I was sad about these. One in a dull silk, patterned with a kaleidoscopic shattered glass print, I no longer had the heft to hold up. And the other—a boned, clever corset made of a heavy and stretchy fabric—now looked empty in its well-formed cups, when once it did me proud. But other pieces fit even better than they had before, and looked different; more flattering somehow, I now felt, on my new shape.

After the initial three months of pregnancy, I had virtually sworn off clothes shopping. It just made me too, too sad to see such beautiful things, released for the new season, which I couldn't fit into, or do proper justice to if I could. Pure torture, for the likes of me. It didn't seem worth risking the purchase of any new things, so it had been well over a year since I'd ventured into my favourite stores.

I can recall well that first trip to buy new clothes again: the first item I bought was a pair of skin-tight silver leggings, ruched up along the sides with many strips of thin elastic. They had a rock star charm I couldn't go past, even if they made me feel a bit muttony, pulling them on and wondering if I was young enough to get away with them any more. *Who cares*, I then thought. I felt lithe and fashionable and thin as I looked at my reflection in the mirror, breathing in.

The second item was a new bra, black, with matching boy-leg knickers, if you please. Soft demi-cups covered in see-through netting lifted me up to a balcony, topped in lace, with a dusky-pink-toned ribbon threaded through and into a bow, same as the knickers. They were saucy, just a little French. I look normal again, I thought, with wonder and relief. I felt inclined to burn the horrible, much-abused nursing ones (although I put them aside in a box, just in case).

Since I had a baby, I have thrown myself into shopping with newfound zeal. And for the first time since I was fifteen, I don't need to buy anything for work; it's all just for myself, so my clothes money now goes towards thoroughly frivolous things. But my new requirements— that items must be easily washable, at least on a delicates setting (no new silk frocks for me … not for a while, at least), and flattering, regardless of the current fashion— mean that my buying options are now more slim. Shopping is simpler, given this.

I have stopped buying so much, because I've far less time to waste; no more afternoons breezily trawling. Now my hunting is restricted to online browsing, and magazine studying. And when I hand over my hard-earned cash it's more of a measured exchange for something I planned hard to buy—rather than an item I spied and took home on a whim from a sale, or in moments of weakness simply because I was there, and got suckered in.

And I am braver, I think. Watching Olive grow—somehow so quickly, enough that a day's passing seems to bring a marked difference—it strikes me how effortlessly time passes. And how truly precious it is. Less crippled by indecision or fear, I am more inclined to reach out and take each opportunity, in fashion terms and otherwise.

—⁓ 30 ⁓—

DESIGNED FOR STYLE, NOT SPEED

I have a theory, albeit flawed: if I could just find the right clothes to work out in, I'd exercise all the time. Seriously. It's a shame that no-one has yet designed the perfect gym outfit for me. They're all too baggy, or lycra-shiny ... the colours garish in the body-sculpting extreme. Of course, if someone *had* designed the right thing, I'd be at it every day! Instead, I use this excuse to avoid exercise for the third week in a row, choosing instead to stay home and cook an elaborate meal.

I went to the butcher the other day, searching for a side of pork to roast, complete with crackling to rub delicious cold-pressed olive oil and sea salt into, and serve with sweet potatoes and parsnip—simply because there was an autumnal chill in the air. Cooking that meal was a last-minute deci-sion, snap-made in the minutes before I'd been ready to walk out the door, gym kit in hand. The butcher asked me what I had planned for the evening.

'Well, I *was* going to the gym,' I told him, 'but I'm going to make a pork roast now instead.'

'You don't need to go to the gym, love,' he said (bless him, but I couldn't help note the soft belly hanging over the belt of his blood-smeared white trousers).

And it's not just the clothes. Running shoes—trainers—all of them are uniformly, plainly ugly, don't you think? They bore me to tears. Horrible and uninspiring as they are, I want to yawn just looking at them; forget conjuring up excitement at whipping out my credit card for a heady purchase of said things! The ones that are best aesthetically are guaranteed to be useless for working up a real sweat in. And how can anyone be expected to train with relish in grey aerated nylon, with white plastic soles? Certainly not me.

I'm not one for doing things by halves. I don't go to the gym only to spend a couple of hours walking idly on the treadmill, gossiping with my neighbour and reading a trashy magazine. When I work out, I want *results*. To feel it the next day in my arms, when I can barely turn the steering wheel because they feel like someone's punched them (even though my car's got automatic steering). To collapse, coma-like, into dreamless sleep an hour after I get home, waking up the next day thoroughly refreshed and with a spring in my step. Bliss.

There is something motivating about wearing the right kind of outfit—for any activity. Old paint-splattered yoga pants and a ripped T-shirt just don't cut it. Someone had better come up with something good for me to wear, soon. Time's ticking away, and my stomach's the worse for it.

31

FASHION LOVE FOR ALL

I t's wonderful to come across people who really seem to own their chosen style. I catch glimpses of them often, on the street, browsing the internet, in my line of work, and among my own friends. They catch in my memory, these everyday people who make a real effort to trot out looking spectacular. The girl I went to school with who always exuded a haughty kind of glamour, no matter what she was wearing; the craggy men with rock-star sideburns, dangerous-looking denim, cowboy boots and hangover-hiding dark glasses cruising about in their hotted-up vintage cars; or the sharply dressed older women with striking haircuts and clever jewellery. If you ask me, a very ample dash of confidence, or sass, or whatever you want to call it (I love the Jewish word for this: *chutzpah*), makes up the lion's share of any successful outfit. But I also find them touching, these people who wear their hearts on their sleeves. They're my kin.

These days I am still beguiled by, but certainly less impressed with, well-turned-out celebrities and striking models I see in magazines. I know what make-up, a good stylist, excellent photography, judicious airbrushing and large amounts of money can achieve (although this last point won't necessarily guarantee anyone a degree in—or even degree *of*—style). It's glamour in the true sense of the word; often all smoke and mirrors.

I have some friends in their early fifties who recently invited me to a fundraising dinner with their own friends and acquaintances. Caroline and Dean are the kind of people who surround themselves with interesting types of all ages, so I was not surprised to be sat at a table next to Elizabeth (an elderly, dear friend) and opposite two women, likely to be in their late forties and early sixties respectively, with one of their husbands to my right. It struck me how each one of them had chosen to dress up for the evening. From a natty-looking handkerchief in Mark's breast pocket, his silver hair carefully side-combed, to his wife Cara's chic Anna Wintour-style bob and buttoned-up Shanghai shirt, which she told me she'd had specially made. Verity was wearing a simple white shirt with a striking chunky necklace and bangle, possibly made from shell, which glinted in the low lights. Elizabeth was in her customary chignon, black polo-neck, draped pink cardigan, very little make-up and a pair of Venetian crystal earrings gifted by a friend.

There is a dignity about older people who are happy in their own skin. It just radiates from them, and is unmistakeable. Our cultural obsession with youth seems to me to be all wrong, all topsy-turvy, because surely this is the thing we should be aspiring to? Yes, youth is alluring. The fleeting moment of beauty captured in a perfect, perfectly unlived-in face is attractive. But my money's on the dear old soul with more lines than a fresh exercise book. One thing I am positive of: they could tell me a better story.

32

MY MIU MIU

So, not long ago, I handed in the manuscript for my second book and received an advance instalment, and we had a nice little sum of money just sitting in the bank with no place to go. Our bills were all paid, we had a sensible buffer zone on our mortgage, and had just donated some disposable income to a friend's fundraising activities. The windfall wasn't enough for the 1960s-era vintage Porsche we'd had our eyes upon, or the home renovation we were vaguely planning, and frankly we were bored with saving. The tidy sum cried out to be spent. From the moment we received that money, it started burning a hole in our pockets.

James, god love him, amazing husband that he is, urged me to buy something totally selfish and indulgent. Yes, I am very lucky … believe me, I know it. Surely there are not many husbands who egg on their wives to go shopping. But I think James knows the sensible adage: happy wife, happy life (*ho ho ho*). Plus, he takes vicarious pleasure in seeing me happy.

'You've been going on about a designer bag for years,' he said. 'Go on, do it—get one.'

Now, I know this might not seem true after all I've shared so far about my obsession with clothes, but very rarely do I spend large sums of money on a single item of clothing or on an accessory. Yes, I buy new things often to satisfy the urge to wear something different each day, but this is where my love of recycling comes into the picture and, apart from my solitaire emerald-cut diamond engagement ring, I don't go in for jewels. For new fashion, I wait for the sales or concoct what I want from treasures found in my local flea market (customised to look far more expensive than they really are). I try to be canny, because retail pricing is so arbitrary, and who can really tell you what something is worth, apart from the person who's prepared to pay for it? And there are always far more important things to spend money on. Guilt always gets the better of me.

This said, after a period of being quite careful, I was thoroughly sick of feeling like Second Hand Rose. And, as Otis Redding warned, I certainly was weary of donning the same dress once too often. Or, more to the point, the affordable leather bags and handmade cloth totes I'd been sporting up to this point. They all seemed, suddenly, so unacceptable and not very grown-up. How quickly I'd become bag-weary, given an inch! It was time to embrace the It bag. Or, more precisely, my version of It.

Alors, I started scanning online. First stop? Net-A-Porter.com. Followed by theOutnet, Saks Fifth Avenue and Colette on Paris's rue Saint-Honoré. Pretty quickly I worked out I didn't want black. Too reminiscent of time spent working in an office, and far too sensible.

I wanted a terrific tote I could use every day and, as I no longer schlep the nine-to-five route, that meant I needed to feel comfortable carting it to my local shop on one arm, bouncing *bébé* in the other. A bag that wouldn't look out of place with jeans, but would look similarly at home draped on my lap while I was wearing a chic dress out for a drink. Fun and frivolous, but hardy enough to withstand the weight of must-have items I cart around with me on a day-to-day basis. Definitely leather, and definitely with a decent drop-length on the straps so it could tuck easily under my right shoulder. My rather strict requirements began to consume me. I went bag *loco*. That night a parade of leering, carnivorous totes invaded my dreams. I may have been swallowed by one, entirely whole.

I swear I got a little shiver when I found it. I knew straight away it was mine—*my* bag. This was followed by a much larger shudder when I spied the price tag, but scratch that. I'll share with you Net-A-Porter's breathless endorsement of my beloved ... my Miu Miu.

> Miu Miu's super-soft brown leather studded tote with detachable cross-body strap is a treasure-forever bag for all the seasons. Wear this carry-all trophy piece with all your downtown ensembles for an instant úptown lift.

That's just what I needed—an uptown lift, in downtown Dulwich Hill! I wasn't sure about the trophy description, but of course that's what it was. My little trophy; made to make me feel there was something I had won.

Not one to make a rash decision, I set about looking at every designer bag available from fashion capitals good and great before making a final choice. I undertook my research with the zeal of a good doctor searching for a cancer cure but, sadly, the similarity ends there. My eyes became even more myopic from all the online trawling. An Alexander McQueen 'Madras' tote seduced from the gaudy pages of theOutnet, almost 70 per cent off. Who needs a sale with such a permissive husband? *Phooey to your sale cast-offs,* I thought. *I'm seizing the fashion moment.* And a rather spectacular coral patent crocodile print 'Bayswater' bag by Mulberry made runner-up on my Net-A-Porter wish-list (*'Tote this delectable style with your day-off denim for a vibrant flash of fruity brights'*). A little too frivolous, she was, and I worried she'd not fit the bill for everyday wear. The Brits definitely still had my number, but it was time to hit the streets for some altogether more tactile investigation.

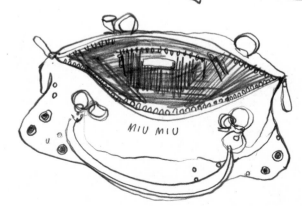

I'm not a big fan of your standard department store; I get a little overwhelmed. Too much stuff, all too closely packed ... and too neglected between customer visits. Not like your average upmarket boutique, where items are lovingly spaced on the racks and shelves and the click-click-clack of coathangers is satisfyingly loud within an almost religious atmosphere (sales assistants and boutique owners the high priestesses of such rarefied spaces). In complete contrast to my flea market jaunts, the thing I appreciate most in boutiques is good editing. That's what you're paying for—someone's trained eye to cleverly

miu miu

separate the wheat from the chaff. To disappear the dross for you. Department stores cater to a wide range of people, but there's far too much choice for my liking. It gives me the fashion equivalent of a computer virus. I come over all funny and shut down.

But I traipsed into the city anyway, to brazen my way through several shops in my brave red flamenco dress with gold trim (for courage), and leather mid-range Francesco Biasia patent black bag slung over one arm. I knew the department stores would be my best chance for covering It-bag terrain quickly. At the David Jones counters I asked politely to see the particular details on a Prada bucket style (pale grey, and far too delicate—I would have scuffed the base and sticky little fingers stained the pretty dove shade to a grubby khaki in no time), and for the purple crocodile skin Yves Saint Laurent to be unshackled for closer inspection, as though I did such things every day. Moschino's postman-style bag enthralled me for a few moments, but the hardware was all too clunky.

I then ventured into Hermès, Louis Vuitton and— holiest of holies—Chanel to admire my reflection with a classic 2.55 clutched casually in one hand, iconic chain straps spilling nonchalantly from my fingers in the mirror. (As an aside, and because I'd so rarely been in there, I was surprised to hear the assistants all still refer- ring to 'Madame'. Good old Coco. I can see her cracking the whip from her heavenly clouds, sabre-thin, keeping up those formidable French standards.) I sighed, and regret- fully returned it to the sales assistants helping me, making a mental note that this would be my next designer bag ...

when the book advances come in six figures. Plus, a 2.55 is hardly the bag you trot out to your local shops for a pint of milk; or at least not to mine, a bit grubby and down-at-heel as they are. I might have to secrete a small revolver in it to deter would-be thieves. That's if anyone believed it to be real. I wasn't entirely sure it would go with my beaten-up ugg boots, that's for sure.

My escape into the fantasy land of Chanel complete (where the Paris runway shows play on a continuous loop), I hopped into a cab and directed the driver towards Paddington to hit the chi-chi boutiques with their smaller selections of covetable handbags. I liked the Marc Jacobs totes but they seemed terribly simple, and terribly easy for a clever Guangzhou leather man to copy. I admired styles from Givenchy and Jamin Puech, but dismissed them as too practical and not practical enough, respectively. And Chloé's current styles seemed to me to be done, done, done.

Back to the city for a double-take on Jimmy Choo. Several blisters later, I collapsed into a chair outside the Ash St Cellars in the CBD's Ivy complex to share a restorative Campari and Spanish tapas with two girlfriends. Relative merits of all bags flashing through my mind, I drowned my chattering thoughts with one too many glasses of red wine and vowed to sleep on it.

The next morning, I made an online beeline back to Net-A-Porter, held my breath and clicked BUY.

Now there is certainly something very lovely about buying an It bag. Several lovely things, actually.

There is the glorious packaging it comes housed in, and its specially made dust cover which you unwrap with glee, anticipating the grand unveiling. (I very near grabbed the massive box from the hands of the smiling courier who delivered it to my front door and ripped it open. Instead, I forced myself to pop it down carefully in the hallway, make myself a pot of tea, clear the kitchen table and prepare for a suitably momentous opening. I might have taken a few happy snaps.)

The swing tags whisper authenticity, and offer up a little spiel evoking dreams of exquisite craftsmanship in a small Milanese studio. There's no denying how special it is to be complimented on your excellent taste almost everywhere you go, although I'm sure that has more to do with the glinting metal Miu Miu label and near-global knowledge of its exorbitant price tag than anything else. I'm stunned by how many people comment on it.

Most lovely, though, is the feeling I've somehow 'arrived'. That I am finally, after years of fairly hard graft, right where I always wanted to be.

This has brought its own unexpected development, not altogether comfortable. I never expected to be embarrassed by the hubris with which I bought my Miu Miu, or want to hide it. But I do, sometimes. It does not do, for example, to claim a refund at Medicare with a Miu Miu in tow. Or haggle over a forty dollar frock at the markets. I also feel utterly fraudulent as I sit there sympathising over tea with a friend who has lost her job in these difficult times, or talk with another friend about his struggle to raise funds to rebuild Cambodian villages decimated by Pol Pot. My bag success feels hollow in these environs. But, like the vast collection of furs I've rescued from op shops all over the world, I've come to the conclusion that the deed is now done. I need to move on and let my Miu Miu live.

And live it does. An inventory of my new bag reveals the following:

✤ one gold leather wallet, a birthday gift from some friends;

✤ one pair of black Karen Walker sunglasses and hard carry case, another indulgence;

✤ a selection of keys on a ring including house, car and post office box;

✤ one chocolate chip muesli bar (in case I'm caught on the hop without food—I can't bear going hungry);

✤ one child-size apricot and bran bar (in case I'm caught on the hop without food for Olive—an altogether scarier prospect, for she is her mother's daughter and bears hunger even less well);

✤ one black and red ladybird-shaped castanet;

✤ one pink wooden rattle;

✤ one pink plastic pony with disturbing rotating head and tail (useless distraction devices);

✤ a half-eaten organic fruit bar in plastic bag ... secreted upon my person for the aforementioned reasons;

✤ one small zippered change purse, the label revealing it to be from Pigott's Store, containing just over five dollars in change;

✤ one Nokia mobile phone and hands-free kit;

✤ a fit-to-burst bronze leather Filofax (yes, I'm old school; I like to write everything down);

✤ an orange and white Penguin Classics paperback—
Raymond Chandler's *The Big Sleep*; and,

✤ a couple of miniature hairclips for Olive's errant fringe.

In this way, my Miu Miu is no different from any other
bag I've ever owned. I'm still piling in way too many things
which will misalign my spine surer than a Kayan tribes-
woman's debilitating neck rings. One of the Miu Miu's
brassy little studs fell off a few weeks ago when I flung it
down rather carelessly. I popped it in my jewellery box and
thought vaguely that I must get it reaffixed, although I'm
fairly certain I never will.

And this is why I bought my Miu Miu, and not the
Chanel 2.55—because I wanted it to be worn and loved.
Wanted something I could use every day and cherish,
because it's there on my person and not on some dust-
gathering shelf. It's why I don't go in for jewels, the kind
you can't wear very often at all, because what's the point
of anything if it's too precious to be seen, to be worn, to
have a life? Buying fashion only to deliberately preserve
it seems a crime, and I can promise you one thing: I will
wear my It bag out. What fun we'll have together, I think.
Miu Miu and me.

~~&~~ 33 ~~&~~

HEAD-TO-TOE

Rarely do I find myself bewitched by a designer's entire seasonal collection. The way it usually goes is this: I see one piece I fall in love with, lust after, seek out, and plot to acquire if it's at all within reason; sometimes a few pieces at most. But no more than that—even from my favourite labels. I might like the whole collection well enough, but I have the feeling that if I go the whole hog (so to speak), I'll end up looking a bit much—a bit like a walking advertisement. I've always thought it's odd to work an entire look constructed by someone else, rather than putting it together individually and really making it your own unique outfit. I enjoy the challenge of mixing favoured new-season pieces with those currently within my wardrobe, along with all my treasured vintage items, to create something entirely *me*. Plus, donning one label head-to-toe is just not very original, even if my budget could stretch to cover the expense. Where's the imagination in it?

But, a few seasons ago, I was left in absolute awe of French designer Isabel Marant's latest collection, having seen the catwalk stills on her website and various pieces filtering down through the trend reports in *Vogue*. I wanted it all. For just a second, I wanted to throw everything I owned away and rebuild my wardrobe in her image—I was hooked.

Until I perused the items in the capsule collections stocked by my favourite boutiques. They seemed the safest picks from Marant's Amazonian lumberjack aesthetic stomping down the catwalk. I was so hoping to make it work—all chunky boots, belt-thin mini-skirts and leather tassels included—by picking a special piece. But somehow, not one single item spoke to me on its own merit; despite being enthralled by the catwalk collection, individual pieces simply didn't translate in the flesh.

I love Marant's catwalk shows; they're not about the spectacle so much as beautifully wearable clothes, and she always seems to capture a look I could willingly adopt, at least in part. But, as much as I fell in love with that whole collection, I felt I wasn't getting enough bang for my buck here at all, given it seemed I needed several items to make even *one* basic piece work (not to mention that I'd have to order many of them from overseas). I wasn't brave enough to take my chances online, and I didn't have the cash anyway. *C'est la vie,* I thought sadly, and searched closer to home for my latest fashion fix.

That was a while back, but this season it's gone and happened again, and I've really done it this time (rather than just thinking about it). I've even surprised myself by buying not one, but twelve pieces from the past two collections by sass & bide. It's rather shocked me. Would I say I'm a sass & bide girl? Not previously. I like their jeans; most people I know have been addicted to them for years. I had a pair of their early indigos in a boot cut which I purchased in London, but when they started pushing the washed-out styles which continued on for many seasons, I lost interest, purely because I'd worked that look in high school and the memories made me shudder. More to the point, my thighs couldn't take the white heat. Their frocks and tops have always looked best on slinky teen models and girls-about-town in their early twenties. With delicate, clingy fabrication, revealing cut-outs, unusual areas of volume, tricksy straps and delicate detailing with beads, studs and sequins, they look spectacularly sexy on boyish girls with beanpole figures—excellent embellishment for those who go straight up and down, rather than those with chicane-like lines. The styles always seemed impossible for one who couldn't dispose of a bra.

But there's something about this particular season which has me in raptures. I was talking about it with an acquaintance over dinner the other night. Both being new mothers, we agreed this season is stellar; a true stand-out. Maybe it's because designers Heidi Middleton and Sarah-Jane Clarke are both mothers themselves now, and have started to make clothes for people with less stick-insect-like figures. Or maybe it's just because it's taken me a while to catch up with their

Sass + Bide
Futuregrand s/s

unique vision. Either way, I love what they're doing. I really could buy every piece, such is my new fanaticism. I'm loving the gothic rock-chick look of Dreamshaky (the latest collection), and *I want* every single damned item of Futuregrand (at the time of writing, in the process of being released), which was inspired by the pair's recent travels to Brazil. Both the ready-to-wear pieces and the diffusion line, Vie—I want it all. It's just bliss, so very fashion and totally now, and also somehow works with child on hip, silver feather charm hanging about my neck, gold and black leather studded cuff at the wrist, leather sandals, and new handbag under my arm. Or on the beach, bizarrely, given all the black, the layering, and the copious embellishment. For years I've been following one of my many mantras: never wear a designer's look from head to toe. But what a *volte-face*.

My first piece, the silver Rats (leggings with elasticated ruching down the sides), had my husband warning there were only a few more years I could 'get away' with them. *Nice*, I thought, but privately agreed. Then I went out the very next weekend and bought a pair in matte black. And a white tee with gold sequins and diamantes, and a funny little black mini-skirt boasting strips of faded grey silk which James refers to as the 'emu skirt', but sass & bide call Colour Burst (ironically, obviously). And a black cap-sleeve bodysuit which goes with everything; another black bodysuit (more of a playsuit, really, with its tiny shorts) sporting glam rock frills at its shoulders and criss-crossing straps at the back; a studded black dress, called We Are Cats, with several pull-strings and spaghetti straps, and which comes with its own little bodysuit to wear underneath; and a snakeskin-print floaty top I'm wearing right now (with the black Rats) as I type this, bra straps and back on display, which somehow just works, even though it's not meant to, dear fashion police.

I keep going back to my favourite sass & bide boutique, the one with all the studded sheep skulls in the windows, panning for more fashion gold. A willowy sales assistant, who couldn't be anything other than a former model, made the mistake of showing me a flip chart of Futuregrand, and offered to put my name down on a list so I'd get a phone call every time a new piece I liked came in. Deadly. I'm already itching for the range to fully arrive and, oops, I just went and bought a singlet with suspender straps hanging down, and A Good Opportunity, the bone print dress. Plus the long Queen of Genius dress with mirrored breastplate, and Don't Look Back fitted knit skirt, with cute ruffled detailing.

It's my new addiction—clearly, I'm in deep. I need to be locked up.

—⟞ 34 ⟝—

NO REGRETS

By the time this book goes to print, no doubt my current look will be passé. By the time this book is a few years old, I'll be working another trend entirely. But right now, in this moment, it says everything I want it to say about who I am and where I've been.

The look I'm working these days makes me feel a bit like a faded rock star, even though it's only in my own lunchtime. Young-ish (at least mentally) and a bit hip, but somewhat dishevelled, my face has new angles and shadows where once plump, soft skin used to be. My puppy fat's long gone, along with the welcome collagen it brings. New motherhood's lack of sleep has made me a little weary, particularly around the eyes, but a liberal slash of my favourite Chanel black kohl makes the lines look like a badge of honour, and more glamorous—more knowing, somehow—than sparkling, clean youth.

My look is a bit edgy, and definitely more 'street' than polished; it's not as determinedly pretty as other phases I've been through, but somehow more womanly. My wardrobe's more cohesive … more complete. Some things actually complement each other now—rather than it being a motley collection of statement pieces—which is a new thing for me. Sartorially, I feel I might just be hitting my prime; I'm finally at the age I was always meant to be.

Another thing: I have come to the realisation that in ten, twenty, thirty years from now, I will lament the loss of my thirty-three-year-old figure, and wish I'd worn shorter hemlines to show off my still-nice-enough legs. Even today I think a little sadly of the pertness of my bosom before nursing my daughter (people were fascinated by my breasts once—now they barely register).

Going forward, I don't want to have any regrets. When I think of myself in my late teens and early twenties, all naïve political statements and downright befuddlement on the rules of cut and proportion (and not yet savvy enough to break them), I wish I'd gone in for more beauty. Fewer experimental hairdos. More glamour. And I wish I'd been more confident, more protective of my health ... and cared a whole lot less about what other people think. But I was smack bang in the middle of the grungy nineties, and living the epitome of the grungy life myself as a poor student-slash-world-traveller-slash-different-priorities kind of girl. My younger self was overly sensitive, and had a lot to prove, something I've now come to accept.

Just a few weeks ago, someone contacted me to be interviewed for a book on motherhood, and what I wish I'd known beforehand. Such as how much of a challenge it is, but also how satisfying, and that I didn't know it would be quite so liberating as it has turned out to be. How it would mark my passing into womanhood, sooner than it might have happened if left to my own devices.

I was asked as well to supply the dorkiest picture that my vanity would allow, to be published alongside the interview. I went hunting through old albums and boxes, dissolving into groans of embarrassment and laughing with amusement at how ridiculous I sometimes looked. Here I am at a party, spinning around, hair in Heidi plaits, with a skirt over jeans, and long-sleeve top under silk chemise ... and in a yellow and pink polyester frock (what was I thinking!?) lining up outside The Tender Trap, a heaving club night in King's Cross we used to frequent in our early twenties, so very desperate to get in.

I spent a whole evening (which carried on until the wee hours) engaged like this, with my husband slumbering beside me on the sofa, finally deciding upon the very most dorky: a yearbook photo from Grade 10, my head cocked to the side and adorned with a bad, cheap, short haircut, in which I look gormless and thin-skinned. Then, only this morning, I ran into an old flatmate I hadn't seen in ten years, which plunged me yet further into my memories and got me thinking about the long journey I've made since.

How do I see myself in fashion times ahead? Spending more money on fewer items, for one thing. I'm moving into that phase now. When Olive is grown and I am her far more respectable *mama*, I will wear more tailoring, and less black around the face to soften the features. I'll still dye my hair blonde (until I die), but allow elegant streaks of grey to show through. And my hemlines will surely come down, at least by an inch or three. I'll sport proper jewellery, perhaps, rather than the leather straps, resin and acrylic I wear now, the fun metallic bangles and rings. Pearls, maybe. Chanel costume jewellery; totally classic pieces, and chunky vintage Kenneth Jay Lane bangles all the way up my arms. Lawrence Vrba and Georg Jensen brooches to adorn a fetching, soft-as-a-baby-lamb wrap, fastened casually around my neck. Many, many scarves. I read an interview once with a supremely stylish woman in her eighties. That formidable *grande dame* said scarves are the staple for her age. Good, I'll start getting serious about my collection now. Accessories will be my thing.

I'll have a drawer full of Wolford bodysuits and silk slips of every length and description, for sucking in or allowing clingy draping; to provide the foundation for good dressing on any occasion, no matter how much the fashion times change. And the perfect shoes for every event, a carefully edited collection of them. Maybe I'll even have most of my things made. Perfect suits and frocks in every shade possible for a classic, chic look. That is my prediction for times ahead.

Although I have to say, the thought of growing old *dis*gracefully holds a certain appeal as well. Who says we have to dress our age? Can't we simply be who we want to be?

Pass me the current issue of *Vogue*, if you please.

ACKNOWLEDGEMENTS

Thank you so much to *Vogue* Australia Editor-in-Chief Kirstie Clements and *Vogue* Features Editor Alexandra Spring for allowing me to reproduce a couple of my articles as chapters here in this book ('A soundtrack to my life' and 'Homemade happiness'), and for giving me the confidence to believe I had anything worth saying about fashion in the first place.

Thank you to my seriously fabulous publishers, Kay Scarlett and Colette Vella, for your constant kindness, talent and support, and for giving me the opportunity to turn my rambling thoughts into a book. Thank you to Amanda Carmen Cromer, my fashion-loving and like-minded editor, and to publicist Shannon Blanchard, who read and showed such enthusiasm for my first draft; you're a dear. Thanks as well go to Kate Fitzgerald, Laura Wilson, Ashlea Wallington, Mary-Jayne House, Scott White and everyone else at Murdoch Books. I think you're the best.

Thank you to Zoë Sadokierski for your gorgeous illustrations; I'm thrilled you said yes to being a part of this project. And to the supremely clever Catherine Milne, whose idea it was to begin with—you are incredible.

Thank you to my large group of girlfriends (an awesome, wonderful bunch of women I am blessed to know and call friends) but particularly Josephine Bryant, Katrina Collett, honorary girlfriend Michael Davis, Rebecca Huntley, Edwina Johnson, April Murdoch, Sonia Palmisano, Lisa Torrance, Jacinta Tynan and Wendy Were, for your humour, support and encouragement during the writing of this book. And to my dear friend Olivier Dupon, for your friendship and humour also. You're my kindred spirits.

And most importantly, thank you to my exceptional husband, James, and our beautiful daughter, Olive Rose. The possibility of my life without you is, quite simply, unthinkable.

—❦ GLOSSARY ❦—

2.55: the iconic quilted leather handbag designed by Coco Chanel and released in February 1955 (hence, 2.55).

Alexander (Lee) McQueen: celebrated British designer known for his avant-garde shows, trailblazing designs and impeccable tailoring.

alpaca: a llama-like animal from South America with long shaggy hair which is very soft and used to make high-quality wool and all sorts of knitted goods.

Anna Piaggi: the eccentric Italian writer and style icon, well known for her signature blue hair and outlandish headgear.

Azzedine Alaïa: the Paris-based Tunisian designer famed for creating the bodycon silhouette in the eighties with his bandage-style dresses. Dubbed the 'King of Cling', Alaïa has enjoyed a revival of late.

Balmain shoulders: the re-invented shoulder-pads style recently epitomised by the French fashion house, Balmain (not to be confused with 1980s Dallas-style numbers: the inspiration is more eighties Michael Jackson than eighties television series).

banana clip: naff eighties hairpiece shaped like a banana which made permed, pouffed-up hair fan out at the back of the head like some sort of lizard frill. In short, a fashion disaster.

bangs: a heavy fringe cut just above or falling over the eyes.

Bermuda shorts: a longish style of dress shorts, originating in the British colonies, that end just above the knees and are worn either with or without cuffs. Traditionally made from a beige cotton drill.

boater: a flat-topped straw hat popularly worn at English regattas (boat races).

Breton top: a stripy style of top first worn by French sailors and elevated to cult fashion status by designer Coco Chanel, who designed and wore one with palazzo pants in the 1930s.

broderie anglaise: fine, open needlework/embroidery adorning white cloth.

Campers: a Spanish brand of shoe best recognised for their flat rubber soles and comfortable fit, before they started bringing out all sorts of covetable new high-heeled styles more recently.

Carolyn Bessette-Kennedy: chic blonde wife of the ill-fated JFK Jnr, who died with her husband in a plane crash in 1999.

Central Saint Martins: one of Britain's most revered art institutions, the London-based college is well known for successful fashion alumni including Alexander McQueen, John Galliano and Luella Bartley.

Chanel N°5 parfum: the legendary perfume with a powdery floral fragrance, first designed in 1921 by Coco Chanel's perfumer, Ernest Beaux, and famously worn by Marilyn Monroe.

cheesecloth: a loose-woven cotton cloth, so called because it can be used to press the excess moisture from cheese during its production.

chinchilla: a rodent similar to a squirrel named after the Chincha people of the Andes and hunted for its soft, velvet-like fur.

chinois: the French word for Chinese.

cocktail hat: a small hat for women most popularly worn in the 1950s; it was often created to match an outfit and decorated with netting or silk flowers.

Comme des Garçons: fashion label founded by the Japanese designer Rei Kawakubo. Kawakubo first made her name with what journalists dubbed 'Hiroshima Chic'—dark-hued clothes with asymmetric cuts, holes, and frayed edges—which debuted in Paris in 1981.

Cuban heels: a type of high heel with a tapered base, not dissimilar to that found on cowboy boots but usually cut away in a more dramatic fashion.

Debbie Harry: American singer and style icon, famous for her white-blonde locks and sizzling sex appeal.

Dinosaur Designs: distinctly Australian jewellery and homewares label created by designers Louise Olsen, Stephen Ormandy and Liane Rossler; has enjoyed success for its handmade designs since it was founded in 1985.

***Dolly* magazine**: Australian fashion magazine aimed at teen and pre-teen girls, which kick-started the careers of many well-known Australian models. Once also a publisher of an extensive range of spin-off romantic novels.

d'Orsay: a style of woman's shoe in which the vamp of the shoe is cut away very close to the toe box, and the sides are cut away to reveal the arch of the foot.

Elsa Schiaparelli: flamboyant Italian fashion designer from the Art Deco period who influenced many modern designers including John Galliano, Alexander McQueen, Jean Paul Gaultier and Yves Saint Laurent. Schiaparelli was renowned for her scandalous designs and favourite shade, Shocking Pink.

Florence Broadhurst: world-famous Australian fabric and wallpaper designer who recently enjoyed a revival when her iconic collections were reissued by Signature Prints.

(Piero) Fornasetti: iconic Italian designer known for his divine prints for wallpaper and upholstery fabric, particularly for his various renderings of the famous soprano Lina Cavalieri's face.

frogging: ornamental braided clasps on a coat, often used in military jackets and attire.

Garance Doré: the world-famous French female fashion photographer, blogger and illustrator. See *garancedore.fr*.

Georg Jensen: much-lauded Danish silversmith best known for his minimal, fluid designs of jewellery and homewares.

gilet: a sleeveless jacket or vest resembling a waistcoat which is usually made of leather or fur.

Givenchy: venerable French fashion house started by couturier Hubert de Givenchy. Designer Riccardo Tisci now sits at the helm.

Hermès: French luxury-goods brand founded in 1837 and best known for its leathergoods, scarves and signature shade of deep orange.

Isadora Duncan: glamorous 1920s American dancer who came undone when her scarf was caught in the wheels of a sports car and choked her to death.

Jak & Jil: insanely chic street-style blog specialising in shoe fetishism. See *jakandjil.com*.

Jean Paul Gaultier: French designer of haute couture known for his shock tactics; has designed costumes for a number of films, as well as for pop stars Madonna and Kylie Minogue.

John Galliano: iconic British fashion designer with his own label and much-lauded collections for Givenchy and Christian Dior.

kaftan: a loose-fitting cotton or silk cloak first worn by the Ottomans and best-loved by modern-day bohemians for its easy, flowing, throw-on charm.

Karen Carpenter: popular seventies singer and member of pop duo The Carpenters, probably best known for the hit song, 'Close to You'.

Karen Walker: cult New Zealand designer known for her effortless, understated clothing range and edgy-cool jewellery and eyewear lines.

Kenneth Jay Lane: costume jeweller responsible for creating fabulous necklaces, rings, bracelets and brooches worn by some of the world's most glamorous women, including Jackie Onassis, Audrey Hepburn, Elizabeth Taylor and Diana Vreeland.

knickerbockers: terribly unflattering style of short, baggy trousers ending just below the knees (mine had cuffs fastened by buttons at the sides). Often worn by golfers in the early twentieth century.

lamé: a gold or silver metallic fibre with a shimmery appearance; often used in eveningwear fabrics and theatrical costumes.

Lawrence/Larry Vrba: designer of opulent and theatrical costume jewellery since the 1960s; his covetable vintage pieces are still considered collectibles.

Liberty prints: a range of mostly floral designs created and released by the Regent Street department store, Liberty of London.

Luella: quirky and quintessentially English label created by designer and former fashion journalist, Luella Bartley. Bartley launched her eponymous label in 1999 with a collection entitled, 'Daddy, I Want a Pony'.

Marianne Faithfull: husky-voiced singer and actress who was a sixties and seventies style icon. Also known for her relationship with Mick Jagger, Faithfull inspired a number of Rolling Stones songs, including the melancholic hit, 'Wild Horses'.

Mary Janes: a type of low-heeled patent leather shoe with a single strap across the instep, fastening at the side.

organza: a delicate, sheer fabric traditionally made from silk.

Ossie Clark: one of the most influential British fashion designers of the sixties and seventies, whose designs were worn by a host of famous women.

Panama hat: a traditional brimmed hat of Ecuadorian origin which is usually made from white straw and adorned with a simple black band around its base. Commonly worn by English and American expats in steamy climates around the globe.

(Sir) Paul Smith: leading British fashion designer known for his menswear collections, colourful stripes and bright design aesthetic.

Paula Yates: perished British television presenter and former partner of singers Sir Bob Geldof and INXS's Michael Hutchence. Yates famously got hitched to Geldof in a red wedding dress.

peasant blouse: a simple, loose-fitting top, usually decorated with pretty embroidery and boasting voluminous sleeves. Think traditional Mexican tops.

Peter Pan collar: a small, flat, round-cornered collar generally, but not always, worn without ties or bows.

Philip Treacy: UK milliner and maker of show-stopping hats; very popular at English weddings and donned religiously by fashion writer and style icon, the late Isabella Blow.

pillbox hat: a small woman's hat with a flat top and sides, famously worn by US First Lady Jacqueline Kennedy in the sixties and copied slavishly throughout the era. A uniform staple on airlines, the pillbox-style hat is still donned by air hostesses around the globe.

Portobello Road: antiques market in London open every Saturday, with stalls running for most of the length of Notting Hill's Portobello Road. Popular with students, fashionistas and It girls alike for its fabulous collections of vintage and second-hand clothing and accessories.

Saba: Australian fashion label originating in Melbourne in 1965; beloved for its simple knitted staples.

Sonia Rykiel: French designer who opened her first boutique on Paris's Left Bank in 1968 and who gained global followers for her spin on chic knitwear.

Stephen Jones: another UK milliner known for his outrageous hat styles; favoured by celebrity clientele Marilyn Manson, Pink, Gwen Stefani, Beyoncé and Alison Goldfrapp.

The Face: cult British magazine which was most popular in the eighties and boasted famed contributors Julie Burchill, Tony Parsons and photographer Juergen Teller; ceased publication in 2004.

The Sartorialist: American fashion photographer and blogger listed by *Time* magazine as one of the Top 100 Design Influencers. See *thesartorialist.blogspot.com*.

tulle: a very fine netting that can be made from a range of fibres; most commonly starched to create veils, voluminous petticoats and ballerinas' tutus.

Twiggy: sixties English model best known for her super-thin limbs and doll-like facial features; recently a judge on Tyra Banks' god-awful yet oddly compelling reality show, *America's Next Top Model*.

Varga/Vargas girls: pin-up-style glamour models, typically depicted in artwork of the forties, fifties and sixties and named after the Peruvian painter, Alberto Vargas.

Vivienne Westwood: legendary British designer who first opened a clothing store in London's World's End in 1971 with her ex-husband (the late Malcolm McLaren) and who designed clothing for punk band The Sex Pistols.

VPL: acronym for 'visible panty line' (hate the word 'panty').

Yohji Yamamoto: Tokyo-born designer of haute couture, renowned for his edgy, avant-garde designs and collaborations with leading brands such as Adidas.